WILLIAM T. HARRIS ON EDUCATION
(in preparation)
Edited by Martin S. Dworkin

THE *EMILE* OF JEAN JACQUES ROUSSEAU
Selections
Translated and Edited by William Boyd

THE MINOR EDUCATIONAL WRITINGS OF
JEAN JACQUES ROUSSEAU
Selected and Translated by William Boyd

PSYCHOLOGY AND THE SCIENCE OF EDUCATION
Selected Writings of Edward L. Thorndike
Edited by Geraldine M. Joncich

THE NEW-ENGLAND PRIMER
Introduction by Paul Leicester Ford

BENJAMIN FRANKLIN ON EDUCATION
Edited by John Hardin Best

THE COLLEGES AND THE PUBLIC
1787–1862
Edited by Theodore Rawson Crane

TRADITIONS OF AFRICAN EDUCATION
Edited by David G. Scanlon

NOAH WEBSTER'S AMERICAN SPELLING BOOK
Introductory Essay by Henry Steele Commager

VITTORINO DA FELTRE
AND OTHER HUMANIST EDUCATORS
By William Harrison Woodward
Foreword by Eugene F. Rice, Jr.

DESIDERIUS ERASMUS
CONCERNING THE AIM AND METHOD OF
EDUCATION
By William Harrison Woodward
Foreword by Craig R. Thompson

JOHN LOCKE ON EDUCATION
Edited by Peter Gay

CATHOLIC EDUCATION IN AMERICA
A Documentary History
Edited by Neil G. McCluskey, S.J.

THE AGE OF THE ACADEMIES
Edited by Theodore R. Sizer

HEALTH, GROWTH, AND HEREDITY
G. Stanley Hall on Natural Education
Edited by Charles E. Strickland and Charles Burgess

Health, Growth, and Heredity

G. STANLEY HALL
ON NATURAL EDUCATION

Edited, with an Introduction and Notes, by
CHARLES E. STRICKLAND *and*
CHARLES BURGESS

CLASSICS IN

No. 23

EDUCATION

TEACHERS COLLEGE PRESS
TEACHERS COLLEGE, COLUMBIA UNIVERSITY
NEW YORK

Library of Congress Catalog Card
Number 65–14291

Printed in the United States of America
by the William Byrd Press, Inc.
Richmond, Virginia

Preface

"In education he made a profound impression on his own generation," Henry D. Sheldon wrote of G. Stanley Hall in 1932. "Because of his personality and of his ideas he influenced the schools of the country more profoundly than any other thinkers except William Torrey Harris and John Dewey." Viewed from the perspective of 1965, Sheldon's is an intriguing appraisal; for of the three only Dewey is still remembered, and he, after all, was active in educational affairs as late as 1952. In part, the eclipse of Harris and Hall may simply attest to the triumph of Pragmatism in American educational thought and practice during the first half of the twentieth century; and in part, it may be nothing more than the eclipse all great men suffer in the years following their withdrawal from public life. Yet there are always specific reasons for the dimming of lustrous reputations, and Professors Strickland and Burgess point to several in the case of Hall.

There is no question of Hall's extraordinary ability: he was an inspired public speaker, an incomparable organizer, and an indefatigable author and editor. Not surprisingly, his naturalistic views on child rearing and pedagogy attracted a wide and influential following, while Clark University under his leadership became a kind of international headquarters for the child-study movement. But psychology soon passed him by, and Edward L. Thorndike was forced to conclude in a biographical memoir prepared for the National Academy of Sciences that "Hall was essentially a literary man rather than a man of science." And as educationists reached for ever greater precision in theory and practice, Hall's extravagance in both realms made him seem a poor model for emulation.

More important, perhaps, Hall's philosophy proved antithetical to some of the deepest commitments of American education. "Hall was neither a conservative nor a liberal," Strickland and Burgess conclude, "for he saw no more hope in holding fast to the status quo than in a forward movement along the traditional lines of democratic faith. Instead, he presented a third possibility, ominously parallel to twentieth-century totalitarianism. Longing for a stable social order under the direction of an elite, and glorifying physical vigor and juvenile idealism over intellect and mature judgment, Hall suggested a retreat from modern life to the national and racial past, with natural education leading the way." It is little wonder that for all his influence in his own time he is little celebrated today. Yet it is this very influence that necessitates our remembering him; for he injected into the mainstream of American educational thought some of the most radical—and I happen to think virulent—doctrines of the twentieth century, and there is no understanding the present apart from his contribution.

LAWRENCE A. CREMIN

Contents

". . . health, growth, and heredity, a pound of which is worth a ton of instruction."

—G. STANLEY HALL

G. Stanley Hall: Prophet of Naturalism

By CHARLES E. STRICKLAND and
CHARLES BURGESS

For several decades before World War I, Granville
Stanley Hall kept large segments of the American scholarly community off balance with a series of startling
pronouncements.[1] This pioneer psychologist possessed a
mind seething with unorthodox ideas, which whirled into
publication and platform oratory at a dazzling speed.
Fourteen books and more than four hundred other pub-
lications raised eyebrows, tempers, and enthusiasm alike,
as Hall spelled out startling theories of childhood, adolescence, senescence, instincts, religion, and human destiny.[2] To some, his work made him "the Edison of

---

[1] Fortunately, Hall left an autobiography, *Life and Confessions of
a Psychologist* (New York: D. Appleton and Co., 1923), but no
satisfactory biography has yet been written. Lorine Pruette's *G. Stanley Hall: A Biography of a Mind* (New York: D. Appleton and Co.,
1926), although valuable for personal anecdotes missing from the
autobiography, attempts no critical estimate of Hall's professional
work and provides no indication of sources used. Briefer personal
accounts of value include Louis N. Wilson's *G. Stanley Hall: A
Sketch* (New York: G. E. Stechert and Co., 1914); William Burnham's
friendly but perceptive comments in *The Psychological Review*,
XXXII (March, 1925), 89–102; and Henry D. Sheldon's objective
summary of Hall's work in higher education in *Dictionary of American Biography*, VIII (1932), 127–130. Merle Curti has discussed
Hall's educational and social philosophy in *The Social Ideas of
American Educators* (New York: Charles Scribner's Sons, 1935),
pp. 396–428.

[2] The most exhaustive bibliography of Hall's published works
contains 439 items and may be found appended to Edward L.

1

psychology," while to others, he ranked "below zero" as a psychologist. According to his contemporaries, he was either "the one really original thinker in psychology in all history," or he "had a peculiar attraction for freaks."[3] In the end, his antagonists seemed to prevail over his disciples. Hall played a seminal role in the fields of child development, child psychology, adolescent psychology, and psychoanalysis; but his writings provided little continuing stimulus for investigation in these areas. Psychologists have seen fit to ignore his theory of recapitulation, to de-emphasize the importance of inheritance and instinct in human motivation, and to repudiate the saltatory concept of emergent adolescence.[4]

Whatever enduring value the historian of psychology may assign to Hall's work, he left an indelible and no less controversial mark on the American schools. He was the chief American exponent of a so-called natural education, or, as it became known to subsequent genera-

---

Thorndike's "Biographical Memoir of Granville Stanley Hall, 1846–1924," in National Academy of Sciences, *Biographical Memoirs*, XII (1928), 155–180. Even this list may be incomplete.

[3] Edwin D. Starbuck, "G. Stanley Hall as a Psychologist," *The Psychological Review*, XXXII (March, 1925), 107–109. Starbuck based this article on a remarkable survey made after Hall's death, in which 167 psychologists offered frank opinions of his work.

[4] Evaluations of Hall's contribution to psychology are provided by Edward L. Thorndike in National Academy of Sciences, *Biographical Memoirs*, XII (1928), 135–154; by Sara Carolyn Fisher in *The American Journal of Psychology*, XXXVI (January, 1925), 1–52; and by Edwin G. Boring in *A History of Experimental Psychology* (2nd ed.; New York: Appleton-Century-Crofts, Inc., 1950), pp. 517–524, 545–546. Arnold Gesell, one of Hall's students, has presented a somewhat more favorable estimate in Edwin G. Boring, *et al.*, eds., *A History of Psychology in Autobiography*, IV (Worcester, Mass.: Clark University Press, 1952), 123–142. Robert E. Grinder and Charles E. Strickland recently attempted an evaluation of Hall's work on adolescent psychology in *The Teachers College Record*, LXIV (February, 1963), 390–399.

tions, the "child-centered school." One thinks in this connection of Colonel Francis W. Parker or, more readily perhaps, of John Dewey; but neither occupied the most strategic position in the emerging crusade for a school adapted to the child's nature. Increasingly during the 1890's, educators respectful of the newer, more scientific approach to psychology looked to Hall. He presided over Clark University, a leading institution in the area of advanced psychological research; and his own reputation in American psychology was probably second only to that of William James. More to the point, Hall's psychological views placed an extraordinary emphasis on the behavior of children, while his social leanings were such that he sought to apply psychology to the problems of the schools. Hall early assumed leadership of the child-study movement, and behind him marched a small army of enthusiastic, if often amateur, investigators, providing what all hoped would be scientific implementation of the child-centered ideal. The father of child study persuaded innumerable American teachers that respect for the "nature and needs of the developing child" should be adopted as an article of faith.

II

Before Hall acquired a commanding position in education and psychology, he entertained the idea of becoming a minister, a fact that may account for the religious zeal with which he approached his many projects for the improvement of the American school. Born in 1846 at Ashfield, in western Massachusetts, Hall longed from adolescence to "do and be something in the world," and for a time the ministry appeared to be the most convenient route of escape from the narrow, agrarian

world in which he was reared.[5] The Hall family was not
wealthy, but with the encouragement of his mother, the
young man acquired an adequate preparation for Williams College, which he entered in 1863. In 1867, Hall
went for a year's work at Union Theological Seminary in
New York City.

The year at Union seriously weakened his religious
orthodoxy, so much, in fact, that a senior professor of
theology forgot to criticize Hall's trial sermon and instead fell on his knees to pray for the young man's soul.
Hall later reported that he "had no taste or aptitude for
parish work, no gift of pulpit oratory, was utterly incompetent and unfurnished mentally to produce the
circa fifty or one hundred edifying sermons per year,
and above all was far too skeptical on the fundamentals
of doctrine to hold my place in any orthodox
church. . . ."[6] He settled on the idea of becoming a college professor and decided to explore the chief contemporary source of heresy, the German universities.
After securing a loan through the assistance of a sympathetic clergyman, the intellectual adventurer left America in the spring of 1868, bound for the first of two
extended periods of study abroad.

Hall's work at the German universities acquainted
him with far more than heretical ideas in theology. The
first period of study, from 1868 to 1871, led him from
theology to philosophy, physiology, physics, and anthropology. Lack of funds drove the young man home, but
while teaching English literature and philosophy at
Antioch College, he became excited about the possibility

[5] "Notes on Early Memories," *The Pedagogical Seminary,* VI
(December, 1899), 597.

[6] *Life and Confessions,* p. 183. Quoted by permission of Appleton-
Century.

of working with the German experimental psychologist, Wilhelm Wundt.[7] In 1876, Hall was diverted by an offer to teach English at Harvard, and the delay afforded him an opportunity to undertake psychological studies under William James. Two years later, he received the first American Ph.D. in psychology, although that honor did not deter him from returning to Germany. He spent the years from 1878 to 1880 working with Wundt and other German scientists at Leipzig.

Studying under Wundt and James had given Hall one of the best possible preparations for a career in scientific psychology, but he found himself trained for a job that did not yet exist. After returning to America in 1880, Hall marked time for two years before he was offered a prize plum—the chair of psychology and pedagogy at the new German-style Johns Hopkins University in Baltimore. There he organized a laboratory and taught such promising students as John Dewey, James McKeen Cattell, and Joseph Jastrow. In 1887, Hall founded *The American Journal of Psychology,* a pioneer organ in the field; and five years later, he played a central role in forming the American Psychological Association. While his own laboratory investigations remained marginal, his zeal for organizing contributed much toward giving American psychology an institutional framework.[8]

[7] Hall reported that he "devoured" the first volume of Wundt's *Grundzüge der physiologischen Psychologie,* published in 1873 (*Life and Confessions,* pp. 199–200).

[8] Both at Johns Hopkins and later at Clark, Hall was surrounded by an enthusiastic group of disciples, who considered him the leading figure in the new American psychology. See the editorial in *The American Journal of Psychology,* VII (1895), 1–8. Gardner Murphy has provided a general survey of the "new" psychology in *Historical Introduction to Modern Psychology* (Rev. ed.; New York: Harcourt, Brace and Co., 1951).

III

Although occupying a position of increasing influence in American psychology, Hall was still seeking an area of research that promised lasting personal satisfaction. His early enthusiasm for Wundt's experimental psychology faded, for the dissaffected theological student chaffed under the limitations of the laboratory and the "narrow" concern with the elements of conscious mind.[9] Looking to construct a psychology that would rival religion and philosophy by addressing itself to cosmic questions about human nature and destiny, Hall turned to Darwinism.

Charles Darwin's contention that man is not a sudden and miraculous creation has since become a commonplace, but the theory created an intellectual upheaval during the years in which Hall was framing an attitude toward psychology. Within three decades after *The Origin of Species* appeared in 1859, the concept of natural, biological evolution had begun to affect every branch of the new social sciences. Even for one less inclined to prophecy than Hall, there could be little doubt that Darwinism would transform the study of psychology. Since no school or field of psychology escaped Darwin's influence, Hall was unique among psychological investigators only in the zeal with which he pursued Darwinian thought and the wholesale manner in which he attempted to apply the principles, methods, and models of evolutionary biology to the province of mind.[10]

[9] Hall elaborated his complaints about Wundt's approach most fully in *Founders of Modern Psychology* (New York: D. Appleton and Co., 1912), especially pp. 313–320, 412–450.

[10] For estimates of the diverse and pervasive impact of Darwin's work on many disciplines, see Stow Persons, ed., *Evolutionary Thought in America* (New Haven, Conn.: Yale University Press, 1950). A more general survey of naturalistic thought from 1865 to

The effect of evolutionary theory on psychology, Hall believed, would be to broaden its scope and increase its depth. The new psychology should be "genetic," and its goal, nothing less than the "description of all developmental stages from the amoeba up."[11] In contending that an amoeba has a mind, Hall had indeed broadened the domain of psychological investigation. He ridiculed those who sought to explain things by their causes nearest in time, and he himself rarely hesitated before plunging into the ocean of man's long history to search for the origins of the more important, because older, elements of human behavior. The result of this endeavor was a psychology preoccupied with heredity and stressing irrational aspects of behavior.[12] Instincts, feelings, and the unconscious, previously neglected, promised to become, through Hall's efforts, a major concern of psychological investigation; and in emphasizing these, Hall served as a bridge in America from Darwin to Sigmund Freud.[13] Heredity, which became a major

1929 can be found in his *American Minds: A History of Ideas* (New York: Henry Holt and Co., 1958), Part IV.

11 "Evolution and Psychology," in American Association for the Advancement of Science, *Fifty Years of Darwinism* (New York: Henry Holt and Co., 1909), p. 252.

12 Hall elaborated and illustrated this concern in two articles: "A Glance at the Phyletic Background of Genetic Psychology," *The American Journal of Psychology*, XIX (April, 1908), 149–212; "What We Owe to the Tree-Life of Our Ape-Like Ancestors," *The Pedagogical Seminary*, XXIII (March, 1916), 94–119.

13 Although Hall disagreed with the founder of psychoanalysis on several fundamental issues, he actively promoted psychoanalytic thought in America by bringing him to the United States for a visit in 1909; and he provided a preface to the American edition of *A General Introduction to Psychoanalysis* (New York: Boni and Liveright, 1920). Lancelot Law Whyte, in *The Unconscious before Freud* (New York: Basic Books, Inc., 1960), discusses the line of thought that influenced Hall and enabled him to arrive at his views independently of Freud.

theme in Hall's writings, accounted for the continued operation of ancient instincts in the present generation of men. Hall argued that acts initially undertaken for survival first became habitual; the habits then entered the soma and were subsequently transmitted by inheritance as instincts.[14]

In addition to the genetic principle, Darwin supplied Hall with a method: the observation of life in its natural surroundings. The great English naturalist himself showed how the observational technique might be transferred from physical form to psychic function in explaining, for example, the similarities between man and the lower animals in the expression of emotions.[15] Hall was suitably impressed by Darwin's effort and resolved to follow his method in preference to more experimental techniques. Although Hall had organized a laboratory at Johns Hopkins, he grew increasingly dissatisfied with experimental approaches. While continuing to support all types of psychological investigation, he himself abandoned the laboratory after leaving Johns Hopkins in 1888.[16]

The theory of psychic recapitulation took its place beside the genetic principle and the observational method as the third element Hall borrowed from biology. His belief that the child, in its development, re-

[14] This view assumed the validity of the doctrine that acquired characteristics can be inherited, a view that lost favor among many biologists after the turn of the century. Hall provided a lengthy discussion of the issue in "A Glance at the Phyletic Background of Genetic Psychology," pp. 167–180.

[15] Charles Darwin, *The Expression of the Emotions in Man and Animals* (New York: D. Appleton and Co., 1873).

[16] See W. H. Burnham's remarks on the nature of psychological research at Clark University in William Story and Louis N. Wilson, eds., *Clark University, 1889–1899* (Worcester, Mass.: Clark University, 1899), pp. 131–132.

traces the cultural evolution of mankind subsequently
damaged his reputation, but during the last thirty years
of the nineteenth century, the theory seemed to hold
exciting possibilities for psychology. In a variety of
forms, the notion of parallel individual and social development had prevailed among many educational theo-
rists, poets, and philosophers.[17] The concept was not
entirely new, therefore, when it found support in the
field of biology and assumed the specific form of the recapitulation theory.

The biological problem to which the recapitulation
theory seemed to provide the solution was the lack of *direct* evidence for the mutability of species. Using rather
scanty comparative data, Darwin argued that man had
emerged from simpler forms of life. More solid evidence that organisms actually evolve from simpler to
more complex forms appeared in the field of embryology. Investigations indicated that the embryos of
higher organisms retrace the forms through which the
species have evolved.[18] The appearance of rudimentary
gill slits in the human fetus, for example, seemed to
establish that early forms of the phylum had once lived
in water. Ernst Haeckel, the famed German disciple of
Darwin, seized on the findings and coined the phrase by
which the process became known: ontogeny is a brief
and rapid recapitulation of phylogeny. Proof of the
Darwinian thesis seemed magnificently illustrated in

[17] Lessing, Rousseau, Herder, Goethe, Fichte, Hegel, Pestalozzi,
Froebel, and Spencer all alluded to some form of the theory. See
John A. Kleinsorge, *Beitraege zur Geschichte der Lehre vom Paral-
lelismus der Individual und der Gesamtentwicklung* (Jena, Germany:
B. Engau, 1900), *passim.*

[18] In 1864, Fritz Mueller, a German biologist, published research
that seemed conclusive. See Erik Nordenskioeld, *The History of
Biology* (New York: Alfred A. Knopf, Inc., 1928), pp. 516–519.

embryonic development, while the embryo also consti-
tuted an open door to man's biological past.

Nothing better illustrates Hall's devotion to biology
than the eagerness with which he attempted to apply
recapitulation theory to post-natal, psychic phenomena.
After the turn of the century, many American psychologists began to suspect that the concept of recapitulation was not as useful as Hall thought it to be.[19] Hall
admitted that all the evidence was not in, but he maintained that research would ultimately establish the validity of the recapitulation theory, which he believed held
enormous possibilities for cultural anthropology. Investigators journeyed among primitive people for clues to
the life of prehistoric man, on the assumption that
"simpler" societies represent earlier stages of human
civilization. Hall welcomed this type of anthropological
expedition, but for himself another opportunity was
revealed by the theory of recapitulation. Why journey
abroad, he asked, when the evidence is right around us?
The infant and child, even in a civilized society, provide a convenient index to the prehistoric mind, for the
infant and child recapitulate the forms of psychic expression that have marked the evolution of mankind.

In 1909, Hall remarked that "from one point of
view, infancy, childhood, and youth are three bunches
of keys to unlock the past history of the race. Many of
the keys, especially those which belong to the oldest
bunch, are lost and others are in all stages of rust and
decay. Many of the phyletic locks which they fit are also
lost or broken." Hall contended, nevertheless, that "if

[19] See Edward L. Thorndike, "The Newest Psychology," *The Educational Review*, XXVIII (October, 1904), 217–227. Doubts about
psychic recapitulation were subsequently heightened when it became increasingly apparent that the process was not as clear and
continuous in embryology itself as Haeckel had assumed.

the goal is still dim and far, it is unmistakable. . . ." By correlating the results of observations of children with those of anthropological investigations, Hall hoped that genetic psychology and anthropology would each throw light on the other, eventually producing "a true natural history of the soul."[20] This large ambition was worthy of a Darwin of the mind! It explains much of Hall's intellectual excitement about child study, which he was so successful in communicating to many of his students. Child study was the very heart of genetic psychology and, to Hall's way of thinking, of all psychology that pretended to a complete explanation of the human mind.

IV

Leading educational spokesmen had urged child study long before Hall entered the field, but no organized effort emerged in America until the 1880's, when the American Social Science Association expressed interest.[21] In 1881, the ASSA gathered information on earlier studies of children and prepared questionnaires as guides for amateur students of the child's physical and mental development. One year later, the association, seeking to become the central agency for child study, made an impressive bid for general support. The pages of its journal hailed the sporadic efforts of predecessors in the

20 "Evolution and Psychology," pp. 263–264.
21 Little is available on the child-study movement. Wayne Dennis has provided a brief sketch of the "Historical Beginnings of Child Psychology" in *The Psychological Bulletin*, XLVI (1949), 224–232. Wilbur Harvey Dutton's unpublished doctoral dissertation, "The Child-Study Movement in America . . ." (Stanford University, 1945), surveys some of the relevant material. Sara Wiltse, a student of Hall, wrote "A Preliminary Sketch of the History of Child Study in America," *The Pedagogical Seminary*, III (October, 1895), 189–212; IV (October, 1896), 111–125.

field, many of which had focused on the study of infants. Words of encouragement came from Wilhelm
Preyer, Bronson Alcott, William T. Harris, and others.
Charles Darwin himself contributed a sketch on the
early growth of his son.[22] Although the ASSA expressed
evident enthusiasm for studies of infants, it attracted
no wide following. Lacking was a dynamic leader who
would dramatize the relevance of child study for Ameri-
cans by making investigations on native soil, and who
would illustrate its usefulness for education by selecting
subjects closer to school age.

Just as the ASSA awakened to the possibilities of child
study, Hall returned from a second stay in Germany,
eager to apply his vast energies and desperate for em-
ployment. He wanted a Harvard professorship in philosophy or psychology, but since he was newly married,
with a child on the way, he was in no position to choose.
Hopeful, he settled near Cambridge, Massachusetts. One
morning in the fall of 1880, Harvard President Charles
W. Eliot rode up to the door, and without bothering to
dismount from his horse, he invited the penniless young
man to give a series of Saturday lectures on pedagogy.

Although the pedagogical lectures were not exactly
what Hall had in mind, they launched his career in educational theory, and through them, he established con-
tacts for an initial adventure in child study. Teachers
and administrators of the Boston public schools attended
the lectures, and through their co-operation, Hall se-
cured permission to undertake a survey of children who
were just entering the first grade. He enlisted the help
of four of the city's kindergarten teachers, who asked
the youngsters about matters previously considered com-

[22] *Journal of Social Science,* XIII (1881), 189; XV (1882), 24-40,
44-48.

mon knowledge among preschool children. Hall wanted
to know, for example, whether the children had ever
seen a cow and whether they could explain the origins
of milk, butter, and wooden objects.[23] Their answers
revealed an ignorance that Hall found startling. "There
is next to nothing of pedagogic value the knowledge of
which it is safe to assume at the outset of school-life," he
concluded.[24] True, the study had an agrarian bias, for
Hall framed the questions in such a way that city children would inevitably prove more ignorant. Yet he was
quite right in observing that with the advent of urbani-
zation, educators could no longer expect children to
come to school with the same knowledge they had had in
the past. Here was a fact with immediate bearing on the
work of the school: if ignorance of a cow amounted to
an educational scandal, as Hall contended it did, then
the teacher would have to acquaint the pupil with cows.

The report, subsequently published as "The Contents of Children's Minds," catapulted its author to
leadership of a movement whose elements were as diverse as those of his own personality. Part scientific
psychologist, part social reformer, and part mystic, Hall
appealed to those who wanted to understand, rescue,
or revere the child. During the 1880's and 1890's, Hall
conducted still other surveys, most of which followed
the pattern of the Boston study. He rarely collected the
data himself. Instead, he prepared lengthy questionnaires and then used his rising reputation before educational forums to secure recruits who did the actual
questioning. Since there was no one professionally

[23] "The Contents of Children's Minds," *The Princeton Review*,
XI (May, 1883), 249–253. Wayne Dennis has reprinted this article in
Readings in the History of Psychology (New York: Appleton-Century-Crofts, 1948), pp. 255–276.
[24] "The Contents of Children's Minds," p. 272.

trained for such work, Hall had to rely heavily on mothers and teachers. The responses to the questionnaires he digested and published, and his articles stimulated the development of child-study clubs, associations, and circles across the nation.[25]

From the beginning, Hall realized that his technique was haphazard and that trained investigators would be needed if child study was to become scientific. An opportunity to recruit talent appeared in 1888, when he became president of Clark University. Hall sought to make the new institution an even more faithful replica of the German model than Johns Hopkins. Initially, there were no undergraduates, so that the full resources of the school could be utilized for graduate study and research. Clark's president arranged that much of the scholarly energy be directed to psychology, which turned out to be largely genetic psychology. Child study had found a home, and a highly respectable one. Hall established a department of pedagogy, and in 1891, he founded *The Pedagogical Seminary*, which was devoted primarily to publishing the results of child study. Men and women enthusiastic about the new "science" flocked to Clark, among them, Lewis Terman and Arnold Gesell. The president himself acted as an intellectual gadfly. Through lectures and a weekly seminar meeting in his home, Hall sought to awaken students to the exciting possibilities for speculation and research that lay within the field of genetic psychology.[26]

By the end of the century, Hall had won for biology and child study a prominent place in psychology. Using

[25] The scope and variety of the child-study movement is suggested in Wiltse's "A Preliminary Sketch of the History of Child Study in America," *passim*.

[26] See Arnold Gesell's comments on Hall's work at Clark in Boring, *et al.*, eds., *A History of Psychology in Autobiography*, IV, 126.

the recapitulation theory as a basic hypothesis and the questionnaire method as the principal technique, Hall and his disciples produced, during the two decades after 1890, a vast body of literature on the emotional, physical, and mental growth of children. Simultaneously, Hall extended his investigations to include the adolescent. His massive two-volume study on that subject appeared in 1904, launching a lasting interest in the adolescent years among many American psychologists and educators. Eventually Hall produced a work on senescence, thus laying claim to scientific knowledge of the entire life cycle.[27]

V

During the 1890's, the child-study movement and its leader became rallying points for many of the forces favoring a "new" education.[28] Sooner or later, most

[27] *Adolescence* (2 vols.; New York: D. Appleton and Co., 1922). *Aspects of Child Life and Education* (Boston: Ginn and Co., 1907) reproduced many of the articles written by Hall and his students.

[28] Lawrence A. Cremin, *The Transformation of the School* (New York: Alfred A. Knopf, Inc., 1961) is indispensable for understanding progressive—or, as it was known in the 1890's, the "new"— education. Curti's *Social Ideas of American Educators,* already cited, provides valuable chapters on Hall and his contemporaries. Richard Hofstadter, *Anti-intellectualism in American Life* (New York: Alfred A. Knopf, Inc., 1963) and Morton White, *Social Thought in America* (New York: The Viking Press, 1947) include highly interpretive treatments of progressive educational thought. The literature on the social, political, and intellectual aspects of Progressivism is vast. Henry F. May, *The End of American Innocence* (New York: Alfred A. Knopf, Inc., 1959) is particularly valuable for suggesting the exuberant faith in human nature that characterized the climate of opinion in which theories of natural education gained currency. Very readable accounts of culture and thought during the Progressive era are: Eric F. Goldman, *Rendezvous with Destiny* (New York: Alfred A. Knopf, Inc., 1952); Henry Steele Commager, *The Ameri-*

complaints about traditional methods and subjects came around to the argument that they ill suited the nature of the child. The president of Clark, who for more than a decade had beaten the drums for natural education, assured the reformers that they were right. He appeared regularly at the gatherings of the National Educational Association, ready to do battle with the "traditionalists." Schoolmen who began to reason that they taught children, not subjects, listened respectfully to the man who seemed to be a walking encyclopedia on the nature of the child. In 1893, Hall and like-minded educators won a major victory when the NEA extended recognition of their work by organizing a phenomenally successful Department of Child Study. On that occasion, Hall exclaimed that "the issues of this hour, which I think the future historian will not forget, lie in this single fact, that unto you is born this day a new Department of Child Study. I am not sure, lusty as this infant is, and visible as I believe it to be, that we shall be likely to overestimate the importance of this event, which gives, as I believe, a new scientific character to education. . . ."[29]

Hall proceeded to specify the details of an ideal schooling based on the results of child study. A speech delivered in 1901, subsequently elaborated in many books and articles, defined natural education in two ways.[30] First, it would "get back to nature," by providing the

---

can Mind (New Haven, Conn.: Yale University Press, 1950); and Richard Hofstadter, The Age of Reform (New York: Alfred A. Knopf, Inc., 1955).

[29] "Child Study," in National Educational Association, Proceedings, 1893, p. 173.

[30] "The Ideal School as Based on Child Study," in National Educational Association, Addresses and Proceedings, 1901, pp. 475–488. Many of Hall's essays on education were reproduced in Educational Problems (2 vols.; New York: D. Appleton and Co., 1911).

child with natural experiences. Hall came to believe that
he could do nothing better for the children of America
than to guarantee them the same kind of life he had
enjoyed as a boy on a Massachusetts farm.[31] Contact with
fresh air and sunshine would, of course, promote the
child's health. Paraphrasing the Biblical injunction, Hall
repeatedly asked, "What shall it profit a child to gain the
world of knowledge and lose his own health?"[32] Hall
constantly reminded schoolmen of their ill-lighted and
badly ventilated classrooms, which unhappily reproduced the worst conditions of city and factory. Beyond
the benefits to health, however, experiences with nature
would develop mind and morals. Throughout his life,
Hall refused to surrender a conviction that "the best
education we can now give in industry, civics, physical
culture, economics, morals and the rest, does not begin
to equal that afforded by the old New England farm as
it existed a few generations ago."[33]

By natural education, Hall also meant schooling

[31] See Hall's "Boy Life in a Massachusetts Country Town Forty
Years Ago," *The Pedagogical Seminary,* XIII (1906), 192–206.

[32] "The Ideal School as Based on Child Study," p. 476.

[33] *Life and Confessions,* p. 177. Quoted by permission of Appleton-
Century. A persistent strain in Hall's work is the preference for a
simple, ordered, agrarian society and the fear that modern America
was becoming too urban, industrial, complex, and chaotic. The
pervasive belief that the agrarian life is superior to the urban is
approached from various angles in Morton and Lucia White, *The
Intellectual versus the City* (Cambridge, Mass.: Harvard University
Press, 1962); Henry Nash Smith, *Virgin Land* (Cambridge, Mass.:
Harvard University Press, 1950); and Merrill D. Peterson, *The
Jefferson Image in the American Mind* (New York: Oxford University Press, 1960). Richard Hofstadter's *The Age of Reform* includes
a discussion of nostalgia during a period of rapid change, but the
best description of the general uneasiness caused by the departure
from a familiar culture is in Samuel P. Hays, *The Response to
Industrialism, 1885–1914* (Chicago: The University of Chicago Press,
1957).

"according to nature," that is, shaped to fit the child. He intended to do more than call the attention of educators to the importance of psychology. Specifically, he believed that the ideal school should adapt itself to the stages of the child's natural growth. Hall's respect for physiological development was such that he looked to it to define the goals of the school as well as the conditions of learning. His major point was that each stage of the child's development is distinct, unique, and inviolable. Pedagogues should not, in their haste to lead the child to maturity, push him too quickly from one stage to another.

Hall's description of an ideal education must have had a familiar ring to his audience. A leisurely schooling, one governed by the timetable of the child's growth, had been a common article of faith among a long line of European pedagogical reformers, including Rousseau, Pestalozzi, Froebel, and Herbart. The child-study movement was, in one sense, merely the realization of the fondest hopes of these great innovators for an education based on a scientific knowledge of the nature of the pupil. Although Hall was never generous in acknowledging intellectual debts to other educators, past or present, he paid explicit homage to the work of Froebel, the founder of the kindergarten; and the American followers of Froebel actively co-operated with Hall in launching the child-study movement.[34] Among his contemporaries, Hall reserved most praise for Colonel Francis W. Parker, who played a prominent role in the "new" education by applying the insights of Pestalozzi, Froebel, and Herbart in the reform of the elementary school.[35]

[34] *Educational Problems*, I, 1–12; *Life and Confessions*, pp. 481–500.

[35] Cremin quotes Hall as stating that he visited Parker's school

What Hall never admitted explicitly, however, was the close parallel between his own thought and that of Jean Jacques Rousseau. It was, in fact, this very parallel that set Hall's work off from the thought of most other reformers of the day. Rousseau's *Émile* is a description of natural education quite close in spirit—and frequently in letter—to Hall's own characterization of the ideal school. The parallel consists not merely in an emphasis on experiences with nature and on the natural growth of the child; using the theory of recapitulation, Hall revived an important notion set forth in *Émile* and obscured or even ignored by Pestalozzi, Froebel, and Herbart. Instead of a gradual and continuous growth from childhood to maturity, Rousseau had detected an abrupt and fundamental alteration in the character of the pupil with the onset of puberty, a change that differentiated the "savage" child from the "civilized" adolescent. In resurrecting this theory of development, Hall even borrowed Rousseau's imagery, describing puberty as a period of "storm and stress" and as a "new birth."[36]

The theory of recapitulation, which provided an explanation of this adolescent trauma, furnished the key to Hall's educational views, just as it had served to unlock his psychological doctrines. Interpreting child development as a repetition of racial history, Hall said that "only here can we hope to find true norms against the tendencies to precocity in home, school, church and civilization generally, and also to establish criteria by which to both diagnose and measure arrest and retardation in the individual and the race."[37] He discovered, first

annually "to set my educational watch" (*The Transformation of the School*, p. 135).

[36] *Adolescence*, I, xiii. Compare Hall's description with Rousseau's discussion of adolescence in *Émile*, Book IV.

[37] *Adolescence*, I, viii.

of all, that children from ages eight to twelve harbor an
instinct of savagery, and that not entirely noble. Hall
contended that these youngsters, who are recapitulating
the life of prehistoric ancestors, are gloriously indifferent to modern, adult concerns because they are literally
aliens, visitors from an earlier age. On the assumption that boys will be savages, Hall pleaded that they
be allowed to behave as such. Outside the classroom,
at least, children should have freedom to run, throw,
fight, hunt, and form "savage reversionary combina-
tions." Conducive to health and learning, these activities
also allow the child to rid himself of uncivilized instincts, thus preparing him for the next stage of development. Inside the classroom, however, Hall insisted on a
regimen of drill, strict discipline, and memorization for
children from ages eight to twelve. This was not the
contradiction it seemed, for Hall argued that "formal"
methods perfectly suit the nature of the juvenile. The
great virtue of traditional schooling had been that it
gave a quick dose of necessary learning without demanding that the child exercise either civilized reason or
civilized morality.

Having equated "natural" with "formal" education,
at least for children from ages eight to twelve, Hall then
reasserted faith in natural development by pinning all
hopes on the adolescent. Hall desired an education that
would be in perfect harmony with the child's nature, but
he was also eager to prove to the skeptical that catering
to the child's needs and interests would not lead to
anarchy. The product of a natural education would be a
well-adjusted, fully socialized adult. Hall believed that
nature would reward the patient moralist by lifting most
children to the stage of civilization at the beginning of
puberty; this would complete the journey of recapitula-

tion. Echoing Rousseau, Hall said that "adolescence is a new birth, for the higher and more completely human traits are now born." The changes brought about by puberty are both abrupt and complete, Hall argued, and the recapitulation process is the cause of these changes. In a passage that characterized his view of adolescence in the eyes of future psychologists, Hall explained that "development is less gradual and more saltatory, suggestive of some ancient period of storm and stress when old moorings were broken and a higher level attained."[38]

Adolescence supplied voluminous detail on the changes underlying youthful "storm and stress." The physiological eruptions that initiate puberty, however, were ultimately less important to Hall than the resulting upheavals in character. Sentiments worthy of a civilized man, so utterly lacking in the child, flower when he reaches twelve or thirteen, according to Hall's scheme. He explained that youth are extremely sensitive and idealistic, and thus responsive to adult concerns and receptive to ideas. The moralist may safely appeal to individual interests at this stage because these interests are fundamentally in tune with the goals of society itself. Hall believed, therefore, that the high school rather than the elementary school provided the proper setting for such "progressive" innovations as allowing the students a good deal of freedom in the selection of methods and goals. High-school teachers could relax emphasis on drill and discipline, provide more "content" and less "form," and, above all, appeal to the students' hunger to be of service to others. Hall's hopes for the future rested on the ability of the high school to capture the imagination of youth and to enlist its energies. Hall further believed that the high school

[38] *Ibid.,* p. xiii.

could perform this critical role in social evolution only if it freed itself from domination by the college. As long as it was restricted to the rather limited task of preparing students to pass college entrance examinations, it could never become a true "people's college," serving both the interests of youth and the future needs of society.[39]

Hall's interpretation of natural education corresponded little with later images of the child-centered school. True, his emphasis on healthy physical and emotional growth in an environment of leisure was echoed in the more advanced educational theories of the Jazz Age. Nevertheless, his program of drill in the elementary school and social indoctrination in the high school had little in common with the principles of creative artistic and intellectual expression.[40] As he interpreted naturalism in education, it was an aggressively nonintellectual, if not anti-intellectual, doctrine. Disdaining a balance in human development, Hall sought a radical shift of emphasis to "health, growth, and heredity, a pound of which is worth a ton of instruction."[41] He offered no new definition of intelligence, believing that intellectual cultivation meant what it generally implied to schoolmen of the nineteenth century, namely, the discipline of faculties brought about by exposure to such "solid" subjects as the classical languages and

[39] "The High School as the People's College," in National Educational Association, *Addresses and Proceedings, 1902,* pp. 260–268.

[40] See Margaret Naumburg, *The Child and the World* (New York: Harcourt, Brace and Co., 1928) and Harold Rugg and Ann Shumaker, *The Child-Centered School* (Yonkers-on-Hudson, N.Y.: World Book Co., 1928).

[41] "The Ideal School as Based on Child Study," p. 475. Richard Hofstadter, in *Anti-intellectualism in American Life,* Part V, touches on this aspect of Hall's thought, but he offers an interpretation at variance with the one presented here.

mathematics. The point of the newer education, Hall contended, was not that it introduced a new way of thinking but that it placed much less emphasis on thinking of any kind.

Hall's determination to de-emphasize intellectual development was prompted in part by a solicitude for the health and happiness of children. To this laudable concern, however, he joined a fundamental distrust of the masses. The public schools were, after all, for the common man, and Hall could not bring himself to believe that the common man could really think. The policy laid down in 1893 by the Committee of Ten, which declared that academic subjects could benefit high-school students whether they went on to college or not, drew heavy fire from Hall. In 1904, he charged that "this principle does not apply to the great army of incapables, shading down to those who should be in schools for dullards or subnormal children, for whose mental development heredity decrees a slow pace and early arrest, and for whom by general consent both studies and methods must be different."[42]

Only an elite could ever hope to live the life of the mind, in Hall's view; and he demanded that "gifted children" be given more attention. Educators would find this difficult if, as he also urged, the school directed its attention primarily to average children, who require release from the demands of intellect. For them, Hall prescribed schooling that would call into play their muscles, emotions, and will more than their intelligence. The

[42] *Adolescence*, II, 510. Hall's doubts about popular intelligence as the foundation for social decision-making anticipated a movement of thought that came to dominate a substantial body of political theory by the end of World War I. See Rush Welter, *Popular Education and Democratic Thought in America* (New York: Columbia University Press, 1962), especially Chapter 18.

seeming contradiction between Hall's plans for the
gifted and for the masses sprang from his firm commitment to universal schooling. Whatever difficulties mass
education introduced, Hall maintained, all children must
be either cared for or schooled.[43] He did not revive older
attacks on the common-school ideal, for he shared fully
the American faith that universal education would somehow prove a means to social salvation. Instead, he introduced a more modern critique of democratic theory,
calling into question what would be taught the masses
rather than challenging their right to be taught at all.
Training good parents, efficient workers, and loyal citizens was the major task of the public school and, given
the limitations of most men, the best that could be hoped
for.

VI

The years since Hall's death in 1924 have dealt harshly
with his reputation in education, largely because of his
failings as a psychologist. One investigator has suggested
that Hall lost authority in part because his catholic interests ran afoul of a narrow bias among American psychologists toward problems involving learning and conditioning.[44] Whatever the truth of this proposition, it
must be said that Hall's reputation suffered much from
his own uncritical enthusiasm. Psychologists may readily
admit Hall's influence on their discipline and grant that

[43] Hall toyed with the idea of infanticide but later modified his
position, deciding that care, not destruction, of mental and physical
defectives was the better social policy. See "Pity," *The American
Journal of Psychology*, XI (July, 1900), 590–591 (with F. H. Saun-
ders); *Adolescence*, I, 394–395; and *Educational Problems*, II, 76–78.
[44] See Arnold Gesell's comments in Boring, *et al.*, eds., *A History
of Psychology in Autobiography*, IV, 140.

he was among the first to suspect the richness and enormous variety of knowledge that would emerge when Darwinism was brought to bear on the study of mind. But even in areas that he opened up for investigation, such as heredity, instinct, maturation, and the unconscious, the most promising research soon passed to other more disciplined minds. Hall's cast of thought was betrayed by his writing, which is all too frequently marred by lengthy, rambling, Teutonic sentences, complicated by esoteric terms, irrelevant scientific technicalities, and blatant contradictions. Seeking to provide in child study a marvelous synthesis of all psychological knowledge, Hall seized on almost any new idea that captured his fancy in philosophy, literature, biology, sociology, anthropology, and all the emerging fields of modern psychology. The resulting mixture awed many of Hall's contemporaries, but he might have had a greater impact on later generations if he had attempted less.

Critics of Hall's educational ideas rarely referred to his social philosophy, perhaps because he made no systematic attempt to summarize his social views until late in life. It was in this area, however, that Hall raised questions of most persistent relevance to education. Although the doctrines of naturalism do not logically conflict with democratic individualism, it is worth noting that Hall felt the necessity for choosing between a school that would produce happy and healthy men and one that would turn out free and responsible citizens. He chose the former and in so doing offered a point of view rarely heard in American educational forums. Hall was neither a conservative nor a liberal, for he saw no more hope in holding fast to the status quo than in a forward movement along the traditional lines of democratic faith. Instead, he presented a third possibility, ominously parallel to twentieth-century totalitarianism. Longing for a stable social order under the direction of an elite, and glorifying physical vigor and juvenile idealism over intellect and mature judgment, Hall suggested a retreat from modern life to the national and racial past, with natural education leading the way. This past may have existed only in Hall's fertile imagination, but his effort to turn back the clock raised in dramatic form the problem of retaining democratic social and political institutions amidst the complexities of modern existence. Hall's concern with that problem, if not his proposed solution, claims our sympathy and gives his writings a relevance peculiar to the Age of Anxiety.

I

Evolution and Psychology

". . . everything in the present psychological situation cries out for a new
Darwin of the mind."

1. Life and Confessions*

Although Hall was subjected to a good deal of harsh criticism during his lifetime, in the end he proved to be his own best judge. In the first of the three passages taken from his autobiography, he describes with some detachment his mystical enthusiasm for evolutionary biology as a basis for scientific psychology. As the second passage reveals, biological psychology supported Hall's belief that a psychologist should experience life "in the raw," particularly in its more bizarre aspects. Hall could treat his youthful excesses with amusement, but he clung to the conviction that his basic insights had been essentially correct. The third selection indicates that Hall found difficult the loneliness and the controversy that his work engendered; but criticism seemed only to heighten the sense of prophecy that arose from his belief that he had glimpsed in biological psychology some hint of man's destiny.

As soon as I first heard it in my youth I think I must have been almost hypnotized by the word "evolution," which was music to my ear and seemed to fit my mouth better than any other. I cannot conceive why I seemed thus predisposed to an interest in everything that could be brought under that term. Of course on the farm I was

* *Life and Confessions of a Psychologist* (New York: Copyright, 1923, by D. Appleton and Co.; renewed, 1951), pp. 357–363, 578–580, 594–596. By permission of Appleton-Century.

constantly realizing that everything animate grew, but every country boy knew this. As a lad my mother remembered that I had been rather unusually inquisitive about the origin of babies, as indeed every child is more or less at the same period; and I used to ask if God, whom I always conceived as an old man, had ever been a baby, and the same of the devil. I think my curiosity somehow got an early tilt toward origins, and even in college I brought much censure upon myself by advocating the view that man had sprung from apehood. Myths and fairy tales of metamorphosis, too, had a fascination. One of my boyish collections was of seeds of every kind I could gather and one of my most frequent marvelings was at their potency to become complete plants or trees. I often looked for embryos among the entrails of animals butchered on the farm and of birds and beasts I shot. I wrote a crude college essay on the nebular hypothesis and was immensely impressed by my first sight of the Hitchcock saurians in the Amherst museum, so much so that I was stimulated to dabble in paleontology.

But it was in the field of philosophy that this *penchant* found its first deployment. For my German teacher, Trendelenberg, as I have said, *werden* or "becoming" was the prime category and the mother of all others, and this helped to predispose me to accept all I could understand of the Hegelian logic, in which all innate ideas evolve by an inner necessity from those that precede, by his three steps—thesis, antithesis, synthesis—which gave the key not only to his history of philosophy but to his philosophy of history, as God coming to consciousness in man. To conceive the Divine as a system of ganglia of reason which underlay and shaped all things seemed to me the consummation of philosophic endeavor. Schelling's system in my mind ranked next because it treated all organic and even inorganic nature as steps in the unfoldment of a mighty process. Matter was sleeping mind. Mind was matter awakened, and vegetable and animal life and mind showed the stages of this awakening. Thus there was a kind of mystic, poetic stage of prelusion by which Darwin, Huxley, Spencer, Haeckel, and even Tyndall were, it seemed to me, prepared for in my philosophic history, and when these latter loomed large upon my horizon they were devoured with the utmost avidity. This was a stage of my development that was perhaps most rapid during the Antioch period, at which also I became most deeply interested and read most widely in the higher criticism which began with the Tübingen school.

To conceive the whole world, material and spiritual, as an organic unity, to eliminate all breaks and supernaturalism, and to realize that everything within and without was hoary with age, so that in most experiences we were dealing only with the topmost twigs of vast but deeply buried trees, gave me a totally new aspect of life. Inconsistencies troubled me little but I was everywhere in avid quest of illustrations of developmental stages to span all chasms, and I conceived all creative processes as still active, all about me, and above all felt that there was nothing really dead but that there was everywhere life abounding, filling all possibilities everywhere, which gave and still gives the deepest intellectual satisfaction that I have ever known. I was bat-eyed to difficulties and impatient at objections, and had a blind spot in my mind for every break in the developmental order and implicit faith that if there anywhere seemed to be gaps it was only because we lacked adequate knowledge. Somehow, sometime it would be proved to the silencing of all doubters that all worlds and all in them had developed very gradually and by an inner and unremitting impulsion from cosmic mist and nebulae—and perhaps even this would be resolved into something more primitive—while all religions, gods, heavens, immortalities, were made by mansoul, of which a perfect God was perhaps the noblest creation; that man sprang from primeval amoeba of which chemistry would some time tell us the origin and perhaps be able to reproduce; that every human institution, organization, and even science itself were but the unfoldment of infantile impulses in man, the sources of which could be traced back to the very dawn of the psyche in the lowest forms of animal life; that spontaneous generation, although not proved, must somehow be true; that life had a chemical basis; and that perhaps even atoms, like Haeckel's plastidules, had souls of which the human psyche was only an aggregation. And I could even sympathize with Fechner's dreameries about souls of molecules, plants, and planets.

In the days when my interest in child study was at its height I was once introduced to an audience by an overzealous friend as the Darwin of the mind, and extravagant and absurd as I knew this to be, it gave me more inner satisfaction than any compliment ever paid me by the most perfervid friend. To contribute ever so little to introduce evolutionary concepts into psychology, where they were practically unknown, and to advance the view that there were just as many rudiments and vestiges in our psychic activity and make-up as in our bodies and that the former was just as much a product of slow evolutionary tendencies as the latter, comprised about all my insights and ambitions. Along with this went an ever deepening realization that psychology had felt the influence of Darwinism vastly less than any other science that dealt with life; that it lived, moved, and had its being in a preëvolutionary age; that genetic studies here were not appreciated; and that psychological orthodoxy had no scintilla of interest in the ulterior and to me ever recurring problem of how psychic traits and trends arose in the phylum or even in the individual. The study of a cross-section of the mature mind and a description of how it responded to the general incitements of the environment or even to the controlled conditions of the laboratory, valuable and interesting as these were, seemed to me only the first stages of any inquiry and to be applicable only to a very small part of psychic life.

I was also early impressed with the very fruitful conception that psychic degenerations could never be completely understood unless we also considered them as always involving more or less devolutionary changes; that instincts, feelings, emotions, and sentiments were vastly older and more all-determining than the intellect; and that scientific psychology was becoming more and more prone to flout the good old Aristotelian dictum to the effect that it was only affectation to treat any subject by more exact methods than the subject matter required. Hence I felt that laboratory psychology had been influenced too much by the exact physical sciences and not enough by biology, not only in its quest for psychic elements by analyzing controlled experience in the laboratory but also by hypermethodic mathematical treatment of its findings, which should have laid to heart more than it did the results that had sprung from the collapse of Herbartian and later the Fechnerian equations. From this point of view, too, it seemed that the importance being attached to the differences between structural and functional had been overestimated and that in this respect, as in so many others, psychology had emancipated itself from metaphysics hardly more than the psychic

researchers had from the religious problem of the per-
durability of the soul after death. It seemed to me just
as necessary for a scientific psychology to be as independent of the questions of philosophy as the latter had so
effectively sought to free itself from theological influences. From this standpoint I always had a very warm
interest, too, in the Comtean hierarchy of sciences, and
I confess to a warm side always for even the radical
reconstructions of sociology laid down in his *Politique
Positive* and his worship of the intuitive elements of the
soul, which he found best embodied in *Das Ewige
Weibliche*.

With such *apperçus* I naturally felt profoundly that
the taboo which the Church and many higher educational institutions laid upon the teaching of evolution
was hardly less than an emasculation of the ephebic
mind. It interdicted the application of the greatest intellectual stimulus of the modern age. It conducted
youth through its most active nascent stages of growth
up to maturity sheltered from the most stimulating of
all modern culture influences and brought it into active
life crippled and deformed. I felt that biology in its
large scientific aspect and with its rich practical results
for hygiene and mental, moral, and physical regimen and
its immense perspective and unprecedented spur, ought
to be taught in every high school, and it seemed to me
anticultural, mechanical, and even materialistic to have
made, as we did, physics the door through which young
people entered the vast temple of science. It seemed to
me a culture calamity without precedent that the enthusiasm that every able and trained mind the world over
felt for evolution, which was really their confessed or
unconfessed religion, was not encouraged to spread its
benign infection wherever adolescents were taught, for

where it had free course it brought an *éclaircissement* from which so many dated the birth of a new intellectual life. I believed that the culture historian of the future would rank the ban now being placed upon the teaching of evolution as no whit less noxious, if not in a sense more so, than the interdiction of the church upon science at its dawn. It even seemed to me that evolution rightly and broadly interpreted gave a new basis for democracy and government of, for, and by the people because the basal assumption of this political ideal is that the folk-soul can be trusted, and this trust can never be complete until we fully realize that everything great and good in the world, including religion, science, and the social and industrial order, has sprung out of the unfathomable depths of human nature.

. . .

And now I must confess, if I am to maintain the frankness with which I entered upon this life-survey, to a trait of which even my intimates never knew the strength or manifold expressions, namely, a love for glimpsing at first hand the raw side of human life. I have never missed an opportunity to attend a prize fight if I could do so unknown and away from home, so that I have seen most of the noted pugilists of my generation in action and felt the unique thrill at these encounters. Thrice I have taken *privatissime* dancing lessons from experts sworn to secrecy, and tried to learn the steps of ancient and some of the tabooed modern terpsichorean performances—just enough to know the feel of them—up to some six years ago, although I have always been known as a nondancer. In many American and especially in foreign cities (Paris, where vice was most sophisticated; London, where it was coarsest; Vienna, which I thought the worst of all; Berlin, New York, San Francisco) I found, generally through hotel clerks, a guide to take me through the underworld by night to catch its psychological flavor, and once in a den of Apaches in Paris we were assaulted and had, I fancy, a rather narrow escape. In some of these resorts even police escorts dared not go without removing their badge of office, while in other dens no outsider would venture without an escort ostentatiously official. In these excursions I have seen some of the most bestial traits of which morbid and depraved human nature is capable, and heard of even worse.

In the two weeks I once spent at an asylum for the blind I blindfolded myself for an entire day to realize how it seemed to be without sight. Again, I learned the deaf mute alphabet to get closer to the inmates of an institution for these defectives; have seen three executions; attended countless police courts; visited many reform schools, poorhouses and pauper lodgings, jails, prisons, houses of correction and refuge for vagrant girls from the street, and many institutions for the insane; have collected photographs and sometimes made the superficial acquaintance of scores of freaks of circus side shows, a topic on which I had planned a memoir; visited morgues and listened to the gruesome tales of their keepers; examined the scores of charred remains of the bodies of those burned in a New York excursion boat and also of those drowned a few years ago in the Chicago river; have had spells of attending the meetings of fanatic religious sects and of revivalists, from Billy Sunday down; have found admission to secret meetings of radicals and revolutionists of various types; and saw much of the social evil in many cities, especially during the period when I was president of the Watch and Ward

Society. In all these excursions to learn how the other half lived I have been far less interested in institutions or organizations and methods than in personalities, and while I have not sought or attained expert knowledge or even attempted to be an authority in any of these domains, I believe that such zests and their indulgence are a necessary part of the preparation of a psychologist or moralist who seeks to understand human nature as it is.

. . .

The dominantly sad note of my life may be designated by one word, isolation. A country farm far from the village; ambition shared by no boys of my age; misunderstood by my father; the fitting school with classmates too advanced and mature for companionship; college, with only a few choice intimates and congenials; the seminary, where I was suspected of heresy, which thus hindered associations or even broke those I had come to prize, as had also happened in my later college course; the years in Europe, where my only friends were foreigners speaking an alien tongue and with no one to advise or counsel; my interest in studies slowly shaping along lines which very few in this country cared for; nearly a score of years after college graduation before permanent and final settlement in the kind of academic chair I wanted; the tragic death of my first wife and six-year-old daughter just after reaching Worcester; the ten years of living alone that followed; the débâcle of my great hopes and plans for Clark University during its third year; the long period of misunderstandings that followed; the uniqueness of our plan which set us more or less apart; some *odium sexicum,* which began with the publication of my *Adolescence* and was intensified by my

introduction of Freudianism into this country and by my
teaching some of its essentials, although with great res-
ervations (a topic still practically taboo by the American
Psychological Association, which was organized in my
house and of which I was the first president); some acute
experiences with the *odium theologicum* which followed
the publication of my *Jesus, the Christ, in the Light of
Psychology;* my genetic conception of the human soul as
a product of evolution like the body; the crust of diffidence that always had to be broken through at every
public appearance; the incessant danger that if this is
broken I be negative and give offense by somewhat excessive antagonisms; the disappointments about the Children's Institute—all these handicaps gave me a deep
feeling that I had never quite done justice to myself.
This, too, may account in some degree for my yet very
strong youthful ambition, despite the handicap of age,
to finish before I die the work along not one but several
of the above lines I have already given so much time and
labor to, and thus round out my life by doing a few
things which shall be better than I have ever yet been
able to do. I never so ardently longed to accomplish
something really worth while in the world as now and
never saw so clearly just what I want to do or felt so
strongly that I can do it if I only have the time and
strength. Yet all the time I know that the Supreme Quel-
ler may at any time now intervene and cut down all these
aspirations as the mower does the last lush crop of rowen
before the snow and ice of winter kill it to its very roots.
Thus lust for mental increases after that of physical
fecundity fails, a phenomenon characteristic of my
stage of life and which I have tried in my *Senescence* to
come to terms with and understand, knowing all the
while that this feeling of a new inspiration is somewhat

falsetto and probably only a symptom. All the while I welcome, cherish it, and will not put it by.

On the other hand, despite all the above, I must count my life as, on the whole, a happy and fortunate one, and that chiefly because I have been very exceptionally able to follow my own inner interests and inclinations. I love my work and have always been able to find solace in it, not only for all the disappointments that I have met but for all the severer blows of fate. This has been almost literally a life preserver. I wonder if any other line of study could have done this as well as psychology, which is in its larger aspects only the study of human nature. Certainly not for me, with my diathesis and life history. From this point of view I am far older than my years for I have laid aside more of the illusions and transcended more of the limitations with which I started than most. In the views I have attained of man, his place in nature, his origin and destiny, I believe I have become a riper product of the present stage of civilization than most of my contemporaries, have outgrown more superstitions, attained clearer insights, and have a deeper sense of peace with myself. I love but perhaps still more pity mankind, groping and stumbling, often slipping backward along the upward Path, which I believe I see just as clearly as Jesus or Buddha did, the two greatest souls that ever walked this earth and whom I supremely revere. If my intellectual interests have been in the past and present, my heart lives in the future and in this sense I am younger than youth itself, the nature of which I would chiefly understand and appeal to. Thus I find even a kind of second childhood in age more charming than the first ever began to be. Hence I believe I have achieved another new birth superimposed on that of adolescence.

2.   Evolution and Psychology*

The fiftieth anniversary of the publication of The Origin of Species *occasioned many evaluations of the book's influence on the biological and social sciences. Before a meeting of scientists, Hall acknowledged a deep debt to Charles Darwin and called for a similar synthesis of all psychological phenomena. The speech, which is the best summary of Hall's own psychological principles, suggests that genetic psychology in general and child psychology in particular provide the most promising point of departure, with the theory of psychic recapitulation serving as a unifying concept.*

DARWIN'S CONTRIBUTION TO PSYCHOLOGY

The contributions of Darwin to psychology have not been adequately recognized. Not only in his famous seventh chapter on "Instinct" in the *Origin of Species;* in the second and third in the *Descent of Man,* comparing the psychic powers of men and animals; in his *Expressions of Emotions,* and in *Domestication,* but sometimes in other works, he not only showed a depth of insight into, but laid anew the foundations of, genetic as well as comparative psychology. These should, and I believe will, eventually make him regarded as hardly less

* American Association for the Advancement of Science, *Fifty Years of Darwinism* (New York: Henry Holt and Co., 1909), pp. 251–256, 260–267. By permission of Holt, Rinehart and Winston.

the founder of a new departure in this field than in that of classification, form, and structure. For him the soul of man is no whit less the offspring of that of animals than is his body. Our psychic powers are new dispensations of theirs. The ascending series of gradations is no more broken for the psyche than for the soma. The gaps are no wider or more numerous from the lowest to the highest in the one than in the other. The affinities and analogies are as close, and the soul inherits as much from our venerable, brute forbears as does the body. The rudiments are as numerous and, to those who can rightly interpret them, as significant. From the higher anthropoids, we need to go down the evolutionary stage but a little way to span an interval quite as great as that separating even the existing great apes from the lowest savages.

But Darwin's method is always and everywhere objective and observational, never subjective or introspective. Few who have ever written about the mind of man know or say so little about consciousness, which has spun its Merlin spell of enchantment about our craft and all its works and ways. His language is the concrete facts of life and mind, and not the categories and intuitions that an ingrowing intellect loves to manipulate. The brute soul explains that of man, rather more than man explains the brute; the unconscious explains the conscious and not conversely. He posits a natural history rather than a philosophy of mind. As Steinthal said language could be studied only historically—"Sie ist was sie geworden"—so for Darwin the true, ultimate knowledge of our psyche is the description of all developmental stages from the amoeba up; and those move most surely among the altitudes who have most carefully explored the depths in which the highest human powers originate.

Emotions are best studied in their outward expressions
in gesture, will is investigated by the study of behavior,
intelligence by massed instances of sagacity, and not by
analysis under old rubrics. While he would have welcomed all the illuminating experiments and tests under
controlled conditions, which have lately given us such
a wealth of insight, he would probably have preferred
careful observations of animals afield in their accus-
tomed habitat. Let us psychologists find in this celebra-
tion motivation to re-read his masterful contributions to
our science, for nothing in our perhaps all too copious
literature so grows upon the mind by frequent reperusal;
and thus only shall we profit to the full, as we have been
tardier than the biologists in doing, by the method, direction, and inspiration he so abundantly offers us.

GENETIC SYNTHESIS THE NEED
OF MODERN PSYCHOLOGY

Probably most psychologists in our day accept evolution
in a general way and have only praise for Darwin; yet
I can think of but very few whose interest in the studies
of the soul is predominately [sic] evolutionary or very
much influenced even by Herbert Spencer. Students of
instinct have profited most here, although many of their
studies are made under artificial and highly-specialized
aspects, with too little reference to life history and
habits of the species in the state of nature. The human
mind is, for the most part, now studied introspectively,
not only by the literary psychologists but in the laboratory, which is more and more regarded as a method and
microscope of subjective analysis. Even Wundt approached psychology from the standpoint of physics

and physiology, and his great text-book would have been but very little different had Darwin never lived. The doctrine of apperception and even of feeling, with its recent, labored, introspective discussions of peripheral versus central origin and tri-dimensional theories, very rarely considers any developmental aspects; and this is one reason why, as has lately been so ably pointed out, neither Wundt nor the other standard text-books offer any aid to the student of abnormal psychology or of instinct.

Meanwhile, our science has had a prodigious and sudden horizontal expansion far beyond the old themes and limits. We have a psychology of religion, with a more special literature on such subjects as conversion, atonement, faith, possession, holy spirit, inspiration, immortality, prophecy, prayer, Sabbath, and even the process of dying, sin, and demonology. Then there is the new psychology of crime, under its special rubrics, murder, theft, arson, rape, suicide, fraud, and swindling, with traits of the chief classes of criminals. Hypnotism and suggestion, not to mention ghosts and telepathy, have opened another field. Then we have the psychology of sex in its normal and morbid manifestations, psychic differences, eugenics, and moral prophylaxis. There is the psychology of language, gesture, music, imitation, social instincts, truthfulness, infancy, childhood, adolescence, pedagogy, property, play, genius, and prodigies, sleight-of-hand, advertising, war, second breath, leadership, provincialism, business and panic, psychic epidemics, and many more, not to speak of the long list of admirable studies of exceptional individuals from Helen Keller to Miss Beauchamp, Flournoy's Mlle. Smith, Beers, Monod, and Mrs. Piper. Instead of restricting himself to the classic, old themes of memory, association, logic, freedom of the will, conscience, in more or less academic seclusion and aloofness, the modern psychologist is often consulted by parents, pedagogues, lawyers, legislative committees; lectures before popular audiences; or writes books and articles in a catchy, impressionistic style, with great attention to phrase-making.

Thus, present themes are so absorbing, so many and so new, that if we are not beginning to lose sight of each other, we have lacked time and incentive to keep posted and interested all over the field, until now the task has grown beyond the ability of any one less gifted than Darwin to master details, see perspective, and mosaic items into true, evolutionary order which can alone bring unity into this teeming but now chaotic domain. The material for perhaps the most majestic structure yet reared by science is already quarried. The need of and call for a master builder in this field must, ere long, produce the man. Some of us are already convinced that the human soul in all its power is just as much a product of evolution as the body; but our faith needs to add the knowledge that can only come when all the authentic data are properly grouped. That the impending synthesis must be genetic, not in the prolix and platitudinous sense of Spencer, but with concrete facts as warp and woof, is inevitable if the psychology of the future is to correlate the facts of instinct, of daily human life with all its hot and intense impulses and all its morbid manifestations, and so become the Bible of the soul of man, in a sense our current, fragmentary systems do not dream of—this seems to me to be self-evident.

.   .   .

PSYCHIC "RECAPITULATION"

Hardly less than animal instinct, child psychology, as Darwin in his famous observations on infancy, although not the first was perhaps the third to see, can only be explained on an evolutionary basis. The child, uncivilized and to some extent even savage, is precociously thrust into an environment saturated with adult influences because of language and accumulated grown-up customs, traditions, and ideas; and for this reason as well as because of its intense, imitative propensities tends to be very early stripped of many of its psychic rudiments and recapitulatory traces. Yet the more we know the child, the more clearly do we see the germs of many atavistic tendencies nipped in the bud, though many of them have so long been. There can no longer be any doubt that the human infant not only tends to but occasionally does develop real words that are its own original creation, products of the rudiment of the same instinct in which language took its first rise. This vestige is thus not completely eliminated by the early, mimetic adoption of the speech of the environment. I have collected from the literature over two score of these words which, I believe, can not possibly be explained as imitations, and which have been used consistently by the child for some time and occasionally for a number of years. So in infantile drawing we have undoubted, though dwindling, traces of what Verworn calls the physioplastic stage of paleolithic man, before the idioplastic stage of the neolith, who ceased to draw directly from the object itself but rather copied his own mental image of it. Here, again, a well-recognized phyletic stage has dwindled to little more than a filmy vestige in the modern infant, but is as recognizable as the rudimentary gill-slits in the em-

bryo. The swimming, paddling movements, too, by new-
born infants if supported in tepid water; the wonderful
power to cling and support the weight for a minute or
two during the first few weeks after birth, a power soon
lost but reminscent of arboreal life; the phobias of infants of a few weeks or months seen often in nervous
shudders at the first impressions of fur, big teeth and
eyes; the joy experienced by tossing and other levitation
movements, creeping, and the processes of assuming the
erect position; the very intricate and interesting stages of
the progressive acquirement of the complex sense of
self; the loud cry of the human infant from birth on as
contrasted with the silence of the new-born of other
animals, so eloquent of the early power of the parent to
protect; and for older children fetishisms galore, gangs
corresponding to the primitive tribes, propensity for
hunting, killing, striking with clubs, pounding, stealing,
etc., the sense of the power of the point, edge, string,
and many forms of plays and toys, the nascent sense of
death, and other items far too numerous to even catalogue here—all show that the child is vastly more ancient than the man, and that adulthood is comparatively
a novel structure built upon very antique foundations.
The child is not so much the father of the man as his
very venerable and, in his early stages, half-anthropoid
ancestor. There can no longer be any question that its
rudimentary psychic organs are no whit less numerous
than the half-score of anatomical rudiments that
Wiedersheim enumerates. Perhaps, in general, the traces
of the psychic recapitulation of the history of the race
are most traceable and most unbroken, faint as some of
the traces are. Psycho-genesis, like embryology, shows
many rudiments preserved and developed by being diverted to other than their original uses, although of very
few psychic traits or functions have there been adequate

material methods of record and preservation as structural details are preserved; nevertheless, they follow the same lapidary law and speak a language which, when it is set down and interpreted, is no less clear and certain.

In general, nearly every act, sensation, feeling, will, and thought of the young child tends to be paleopsychic just in proportion as the child is let alone or isolated from the influence of grown-ups, whose presence always tends to the elimination of these archaic elements, and in all cases makes havoc with them, over-repressing some that should have their brief fling, if only on the principle of the Aristotelian catharsis, to give early immunity from the hypertrophy of bestial traits by awakening the next higher powers that repress them in their nascent period; but which, in some environments, are left to grow into faults and then into juvenile crimes, which they are prone to do just in proportion as the order of their nascency is perverted. Thus the problem of a true mentally, esthetically and morally orthopedic education still gropes in the trial and error stage, although not without some progress toward a scientific basis for pedagogy which, if it ever comes, can rest on no other foundation than a well-established embryology of the soul, all the way from eugenics and the psychic states and regimen of pregnancy on to the fully matured nubility of the offspring. Thus, from one point of view, infancy, childhood, and youth are three bunches of keys to unlock the past history of the race. Many of the keys, especially those which belong to the oldest bunch, are lost and others are in all stages of rust and decay. Many of the phyletic locks which they fit are also lost or broken; both locks and keys are often distorted and, to change the figure, the sequences which the race followed are often inverted in the autogenetic processional of growth; but, if the goal is still dim and far, it is unmistakable, and as we slowly and surely approach it, the genetic psychologist feels it beckoning, calling, and inspiring, almost like a new muse. This has introduced a temporal perspective or new dimension into a field where most preceding and even present studies have all been in the flat surface of the present state of adult consciousness. This is supported by, though still but very imperfectly correlated with, the studies of animal instinct on the one hand, and with those of the myth, custom, and belief of primitive races on the other. It already suggests to the many laboratory studies of the affective life (based on the method of controlling the conditions of very slight variations of emotional tone exigously made and based only on a few adult experts), a more excellent way, which would tend to bring psychology back to the study of human life as it is lived out, where it is hottest, most intense and passional with love, anger, fear, hate, jealousy, grim and dour struggles with sin, wrought out with sweat, blood, and supreme effort, with perhaps the life and death of the individual or even the race at stake. Here, rather than in the isolation of the laboratory or the study, lies the heart of a psychology that touches life and that really avails and has worth and value, because it is in line with the eternal powers and is, in a word, a true, natural history of the soul, and can make "philosophy" again, as the motto of one of our best-known culture fraternities has it, "the guide of life."

THE PSYCHOLOGY OF THE FUTURE

Finally, education, now perhaps the most universal and uniform of all the social institutions, is now looking to psychology for guidance as never before, and we are at present able to meet this call in only a halting and partial way. Religion seems of late to be becoming strangely docile to all the too little we have to teach it. Psychiatry, to which we should have at least given a science of normal psychic life, is now in danger of finding our texts of little avail in solving its problems, is building new foundations of its own, and growing weary of our sophistic subtleties concerning parallelism and interaction and the nature of feeling, conscience, etc. Few, even of our recent experimental results, are available for determining or influencing normality or abnormality; our discussions of freedom, necessity, or responsibility are too academic for use in criminology. The great newly discovered continent of the unconscious is still regarded by many members of our guild as mystical, perhaps superliminal, and its phenomena are used to cast auguries as to whether the soul is independent of or survives the body. The unconscious is really like the submerged eight-ninths of an iceberg, which is impelled by deeper currents in a denser medium, and which the glittering summits that emerge above the tide and are impelled by only atmospheric pressure have little control over. And once more, just as psychiatry is now changing its emphasis from a predominantly somatic and neurological basis, which has been so fruitful under the old slogan of Virchow, "Ubi est morbus," to a more psychic, pathological viewpoint, so perhaps even the doctrine of heredity is coming our way by changing the terms applied to its elements from the mystic, pathological ids and determinations of Weismann to Semon's no less mystic but psychological postulates of mnemes and engrams. Here, too, we are hardly ready to meet the new demands or utilize the new principles, because our department is still, despite its great, recent progress, only half scientific and is not unlike Milton's new-born tawny

lion pawing to get away from the metaphysical and theological soil from which it sprang. We have too long
yielded to the seductions of the heterai of the ancient,
speculative problems that have obsessed us and not yet
definitely broken with those in our midst who still urge
that psychology should be developed in the closest rapport with, if not under the influence of, a speculative
philosophy.

Finally, as Darwin freed biology from the inveterate
dominance of the ideas of fixed and divinely created
species, conceptions directly inherited from Plato's ideas
and Aristotle's categories, so everything in the present
psychological situation cries out for a new Darwin of the
mind, who shall break the persistent spell of theoretical
problems incapable of scientific solution, the ideal of a
logical and methodical exactness greater than our subject in its present stage permits of, which Aristotle well
dubbed pedantry, and remand the haunting problem of
the ultimate nature of consciousness and the final goal
of the psyche to the same limbo, by suspending convic-
tions, as those of the constitution or cause of energy
and the nature of reality and objectivity. Only by so doing can we again get up against the essential facts of life
as it is lived out by the toiling, struggling men, women,
and children, normal and defective, of our day. If this
rough diagnosis of the present situation is correct, only
a pessimist can doubt that the need will, ere long, bring
the man or the men to meet it in the only way it can be
met, viz., by a comprehensive evolutionary synthesis in
the psychological domain, which by every token seems at
present to impend.

II

Child Study

"Just as to command inanimate nature we must constantly study, love, obey her, so to control child nature we must first, and perhaps still more piously, study, love, obey it."

3.   The Story of a Sand-Pile*

This description of children at play, one of the most charming pieces Hall ever wrote, demonstrates that he had a keen eye for detail and that he was capable of great sympathy for, and understanding of, childhood. Although this longitudinal study is not typical of Hall's technique, it provides insight into his psychological theory, which came to emphasize developmental factors. Specifically, the report describes the manner in which children, presumably without adult guidance, created their own social institutions. "The Story of a Sand-Pile," which Hall later called an "idyll of recapitulation," seemed to provide evidence that the child's natural development could be taken as the basis for his socialization.

The town of B. is a quiet community of a few score families of farmers, some twenty or thirty miles from Boston. Among the few cottagers who spend the summer months there is the Rev. Dr. A., a professor at Cambridge, Mass., and widely known as an author. The family consists of Mrs. A. and two bright, healthy boys, now fourteen and twelve, whom I will here call, respectively, Harry and Jack. Nine summers ago the mother persisted, not without some inconvenience, in having a load of fine clean sand hauled from a distant beach and

*Scribner's Magazine, III (June, 1888), 690–696.

dumped in the yard for the children to play in. What follows might be called a history of that load of sand, which I will try to sketch in the most literal and unadorned way, as I saw and heard of it, for the sake of its unique educational interest.

The "sand-pile" at once became, as everyone who has read Fröbel or observed childish play would have expected, the one bright focus of attraction, beside which all other boyish interests gradually paled. Wells and tunnels; hills and roads like those in town; islands and capes and bays with imagined water; rough pictures drawn with sticks; scenes half reproduced in the damp, plastic sand and completed in fancy; mines of ore and coal, and quarries of stone, buried to be rediscovered and carted to imaginary markets, and later a more elaborate half-dug and half-stoned species of cave-dwelling or icehouse—beyond such constructions the boys probably did not go for the first summer or two. The first and oldest "house," of which tradition survives, was a board pegged up on edge with another slanted against it, under which toys were taken from the nursery to be sheltered from showers. Next came those made of two bricks and a board. The parents wisely refrained from suggestions, and left the hand and fancy of the boys to educate each other under the tuition of the mysterious play-instinct.

One day a small knot of half-rotten wood was found, a part of which suggested to Harry the eye and head of a horse, and a horse it at once became, though it had nothing to suggest tail or legs. In another artificial horse soon attempted these were represented by roughly whittled projections. Gradually wooden horses, made in spans for firmer standing on uneven ground, held together by a kind of Siamese-twins commissure, to which vehicles could be conveniently attached, were evolved.

These horses are perhaps two inches long, with thread tail and mane, pinhead eyes, and a mere bulb, like the Darwinian protuberance on the infolded margin of the human helix, for an ear. For the last two or three years this form has become rigidly conventionalized, and horses are reproduced by the jigsaw as the needs of the community require, with Chinese fidelity to this pattern. Cows and oxen, with the characteristic distinctions in external form strongly accented, were drawn on paper or pasteboard and then cut or sawn into shape in wood. Those first made proved too small compared with later standards of size, and so were called yearlings and calves, and larger "old steers" and "Vermont spotted cattle" were made. Pigs and sheep came later, poultry alone being still unshapely, hens consisting of mere squares of wood of prescribed size.

There is no further record or memory of the stages of development of this community, for such it soon became by the gradual addition of half a dozen other congenial boys from the neighborhood, and I can only describe the buildings, government, tools, money, trade, laws, men, etc., as I found them. Nearly a dozen farms are laid out on one main and several lesser streets, somewhat like those in town, each, perhaps, five or six feet square, with tiny rows of stone for walls and fences, with pasture and mow-lots, and fields planted with real beans, wheat, oats, and corn, which is topped before it has spindled, and with a vase or box for a flower garden. A prominent feature of these farms is at present the gates, which are admirably mortised and hung, and perhaps represent the high-water mark of skill in wood-work. This unique prominence of a single feature on which attention is concentrated is a typical mark of childish production; as a girl or boy is drawn with buttons, or a hat, or a pocket, or a man with a pipe, or a house with a key-hole, etc., strikingly predominant. The view of this Lilliputian settlement from the road is quite picturesque. Houses and barns are perhaps a foot high, and there is a flagpole, painted and sanded at the base, to prevent the tiny inhabitants from whittling it, with a joint, and cords to raise and lower the flag, and a peg-ladder, the top towering perhaps two feet above the ground. There are pig-pens with quite well-carved troughs, and hen-yards with wire-net fences, and a very undeveloped system of sewerage, suggested by a disastrous shower, and centring in a sunken tomato-can.

Great attention has been bestowed on the barns. On one side are stanchions for cows, with stalls for horses, and others for yoked cattle, and stairs and lofts for hay, and genuine slanting roofs, and doors that clamp and bar inside against horse-thieves. One boy built a cupola and another a windmill, painted in many colors, on his barn, but this fashion did not take. The doors are not large enough for the boys' hands to enter with facility, and so the whole building was made to lift up from its floor on hinges. Hay is cut and dried, and sometimes stored in mows on scaffolds, while poorer hay is stacked out-of-doors about a skewer for a stack-pole. More recently, however, most hay is put up in pressed bales, about one by two inches, for market, or to be kept over for another year. Most other crops that are planted do not come to maturity, and so wheat, beans, corn, oats, etc., are bagged and sold or stored "as if" they had been grown by the seller. In this community, as often in real life in New England, the barn is often far larger, more expensive, and attracts more interest than the house. Only the outsides of the latter are attended to. The youngest boy alone, despite some ridicule for his girlishness, has embellished his house within, and set out moss, and planted flower-beds and vines, without. A young lady visitor thoughtlessly introduced a taste for luxury by painting not only shingles on the roof and bricks into the chimney, but lace curtains into the windows of one house. Another boy-proprietor dug and stoned up a well, made a long sweep and hung it with a counterweight in a natural crotch, and made a bucket of a cherry-stone.

The adult population of this community are men and women about two and a half inches tall, whittled out of wood. The women stand on a base made by their broad skirts, and the men stand on ground, or on carts, etc., by means of a pin projecting from the feet, by which they can be stuck up anywhere. One or both arms are some-times made to move, but otherwise they are very roughly manufactured. They have been kept for years, are named Bill Murphy, Charles Stoughton, Peter Dana, etc., from real men in town, and each have families, etc. Each boy represents one of these families, but more particularly the head of it, whose name he takes, and whom he talks both to and for, nasally, as does the original Bill Murphy, etc. In fact, the personality of the boys is strangely merged in that of these little idols or fetiches. If it is heard that the original Farmer Murphy has done anything disreputable—cheated in a horse-trade, for instance—the other boys reproach or threaten with expulsion the boy who represents the wooden Mur-phy, greatly to his chagrin. The leg of one wooden man was blown off by a toy cannon accidentally, one Fourth of July, and he was given up as dead, but found after some months, and supplied with a new leg by the carpen-ter-doctor. The boys get up at night to bring these men in if they got left out accidentally, keeping them in the house if they catch cold by such exposure, take them along in their pockets if they go to the city or on a pleasure-trip, send them in letters and express packages to distant friends, to be returned, in order that they may be said to have been to this or that place. The best man has travelled most, keeps his farm in best order, has the most joints in his body, keeps dressed in the best coat of paint, and represents the best farmer in town, and is represented by the best boy. The sentiment toward these little figures is more judicial and paternal than that of little girls for dolls. Their smallness seems to add a charm akin to that of largeness in a doll for girls. If a new boy enters the community, or if accident or general consent, or any other cause, requires the production of new men, they are still made roughly after the old patterns, and far below the best skill the boys have now acquired in wood-work. Two years ago, when clothes began to be painted on these figures, those who were created as wage-workers were painted with overalls on. The question at once arose whether these men should be allowed to come into the house with their employers without a change of garments, which involved, of course, a new coat of paint. It was decided that they must live apart by themselves. Thus, the introduction of hired men marked the beginning of a system of castes. The boys' own wishes and thoughts are often, especially if of a kind that involves a little self-consciousness or restraint, expressed by saying half seriously that the little figure wishes to do this, or thinks that, etc. Their supposed relation to one another in the high tide of the play-spirit, dominates the actual relation of the boys to one another, as two little girls who were sisters were overheard saying, "Let's play we are sisters," almost as if the play made that relation more real than the fact.

Prominent among the benefits the "sand-pile" community has brought the boys, is the industrial training it has involved, particularly in wood-work. In this respect preparation for the summer is made to enliven the long Cambridge winters. The evolution of the plough, *e.g.,* is as follows: It began as a rough pointed paddle; then came a pole drawn by the small end with a stiff branch cut long and sharpened, then a rough share, then a metallic point, then two handles, then a knife, etc. Thus, the plough, which fortunately did not get stereotyped early, has passed through a number of stages still to be seen, and is now quite complete in form. In the case of the hoe and ax, wood has supplanted metal because more easily and correctly fashioned. The rake, shovel, pick, harrow, and dray, pitchfork, snow-shovel, ladder, stone-boat, beetle-and-wedge, and gravel-sieve, all show stages of improvement, and sometimes involve some skill in shaping or adapting wire, tin, etc. These tools are very small, and not for the most part adapted to much real use, and quite disproportionately large as compared with the size of houses and men. Milk cans, pulleys, wheel-barrows, carts, wagons, and harnesses are made with still more skill. Harnesses have real collars, hames, bit, bridle, and stringlines. Wagons have wheels (made of a section of a large curtain-stick or of checker-board men), brakes, end-boards, king-bolts, neaps, and shafts, stakes for hay, a high seat for the driver, etc. They can be made to tip up, and include many varieties—as a milk-cart with money-box, a long timber-truck, market wagon, and others. Could the stages of evolution through which a few of these implements of farm-work have passed be pinned on cards in their order of development and photographed they would quite likely reflect in some respects the progress of mankind in their production. It is in connection with these products mainly that a patent office has been proposed, but up to the close of last season not established.

Carpentry has thus proven the most successful industry, and has of late slowly come to be largely the monopoly of Harry, who probably has most skill and the best tools. One boy made a croquet-set of very miniature proportions. Another established brick-works based on a careful study of those in Cambridge; but the products of his yard, though admirably done, have not come into demand as building material. Another attempted moulding and pottery, including baking, but with rather poor success. A tiny newspaper, some three inches square, devoted entirely to the affairs of the "sand-pile" was started, with seven subscribers, at a dollar per month in their peculiar currency, but the labor of duplicating soon caused its abandonment. At one time candles were manufactured in tiny moulds. Two sailing vessels, the Argonaut and Neptune, were made and raced till boom and gaff were broken. Tiny pine-trees were set out, and ash fertilizers prepared and used for crops. The farmers near by go to a distant meadow to cut marsh hay at low tide, and are gone overnight. This the boys parodied with a damp spot of mow-land as a marsh, and over-night—represented by the interval of dinner. Cord-wood of several lengths, with an inch representing a foot, and with both cleft and trash varieties, was cut down, piled, and sold. On one occasion the boys were observed creeping about one-eighth of a mile and back, propelling their tiny horses held between their fingers, each span drawing a cart loaded with their wood. The functions of carpenter and doctor are fused in one, the office of the latter being chiefly to mend broken limbs, splints being used, but the *vis reparatrix* of nature being represented by the drying of glue.

Trade centred in the grocery store, of which Jack was one proprietor, the name of the puppet he represented being painted on the sign. A toy watch was hung in the gable to represent the clock over Faneuil Hall Market, and a clay watch-dog was on guard by night. Cans of pickles were put up; partridge and huckle-berries, in small glass bottles; candy was sold by the barrel; tomatoes were represented by red bar-berries, and water-melons by butternuts. Grass put up in bags for cows and horses was sold by weight on a pair of small scales. Shelves and counters, and a canvas-topped market wagon, were the chief features of this establishment. Its goods were, however, for the most part, in a sense unreal, its business declined until at last its proprietors were obliged to declare themselves bankrupt, and a bill of sale and auction closed its career.

The need of a measure of value and a medium of exchange was felt early in the history of the "sand-pile." A special kind of card-board was procured, and later, as this material was found not to be proof against counterfeiting, a species of felt was used, out of which small ellipsoidal currency was cut with a gouge of peculiar curvature. These coins were of two sizes, representing dollars and half-dollars respectively. At the beginning of the first season ninety dollars and fifty half-dollars were given to each boy, and the gouge and felt, representing mint and bullion, laid away, thus insuring a strictly limited circulation. This currency became so very real that actual silver dollars and half-dollars were said, I know not how correctly, to have been vainly offered for their felt counterparts, the fluctuations in the silver value of which recorded the varying intensity of the play-spirit of the "sand-pile." When the grocer failed he became really a pauper on the community. He was, I think, the young-

est boy, and his monetary ventures had gradually re-
lieved him of his entire capital. He was aided in little
ways, and meetings were held to discuss the best way of
relieving him. One proposition was a general pro-rata
subscription; another was a communistic redistribution
of the money of the community. These schemes were
successfully opposed, however, and it was at last agreed
to inflate their first currency by issuing enough money to
give each boy an additional sum of ten dollars. While
this matter was under discussion, and redistribution was
expected by some, prices were affected, and a few sales
were made at prices so high as to cause embarrassment
later.

Laws were enacted only to meet some pressing necessity. Town meetings were summoned by an elected crier,
who shouted "Ding dong, come to town meeting!" These
assemblages were at first held on and about the fence or
near their hotel, each boy holding his little wooden
dummy in his hand and turning up its arm when ayes or
noes were called. Later a bell and hall were provided.
The officers elected were president, flag-man, whose duty
it was to keep the flag-pole in order and the flag flying, a
pound-keeper to look after stray animals carelessly left
lying about or lost by other boys, a surveyor of roads,
whose duties were sometimes considerable after a
shower, a janitor for the hall, and a sprinkler and
waterer of crops, etc. A scheme of taxation was proposed, but as it was to be based mainly on land, and as
the task of measuring the sometimes irregularly laid out
farms was considerable, it was never carried out. A system of fines was also adopted, the enforcement of which
led to quarrels, and was stopped by parental interven-
tions. A jail and a grog-shop shared a similar fate. So
great was the influence of proceedings in this community

upon the general direction of interest and attention that it was feared that an undesirable degree of knowledge of criminality and intemperance would be fostered if these latter institutions were allowed to develop. It was at these meetings that the size of a cord of wood and an acre of land was settled. Judicial as well as legislative functions appertained to these meetings. After a fire-cracker had blown up a house, a law was passed limiting the proximity to the village at which fireworks should be permissible. A big squirt-gun served as a fire-engine, and trouble was at once imminent as to who should control and use it, till it was enacted that it should be under the control of the boy whose buildings were burning. One boy was tried for beating his horses with a pitchfork, and another for taking down the pound wall and leading out his cattle without paying the fine. Railroads were repeatedly proposed, but never constructed, since the earliest days of the "sand-pile," when they did exist for a short time, for the double reason that they would interfere with teaming, which was on the whole still more interesting, and because every boy would want to be conductor and president of the company.

"Why do you have no church?" the boys were asked. "Because," they replied, "we are not allowed to play in the 'sand-pile' on Sunday, but have to go to church." "And why have you no school?" "Why," said they, exultingly, "it is vacation, and we don't have to go to school."

The geography of the surrounding region is not well developed. The house in which the parents lived is called Cambridge, its piazza is Concord. A gully made by a water-spout is Rowley. Another smaller sand-pile once started near by is West B. A neighbor's house more recent is Vermont. A place where worms are dug for fishing is called Snakeville, and another spot where some Oswego starch-boxes once lay is Oswego. Boston is a neighboring settlement. The topographical imagination of these boys is far less developed than in the case of a group of school-children the writer once knew, who played for years about a marsh half submerged in spots by high tide, and who had named continents, capes, bays, lakes, rivers, islands, promontories, to the number of perhaps several score, from real or fancied resemblance to great features of the world's surface on the map, and who had in a number of cases helped out resemblances by digging, and who carried on a brisk commerce between leading ports for entire summers, and with many details and circumstances of real trade.

The conservatism of Harry and Jack and the boys that gathered about them was shown even in the name "sand-pile," which the whole enterprise still bears. This designation is now entirely inappropriate, for all the sand originally dumped on the spot has been carefully removed and its place filled in with loam. Each spring, when the houses, barns, etc., are brought out and set up, the traditions of the preceding year are carefully observed in laying out the streets. Most boys hold that the monetary relations of the previous year should continue over to the new season, the rich at the close of the last year starting rich this year. This view generally prevails against the theory of an annual year of jubilee, and a release from last year's debts, that the poorer boys uphold. All the boys in town, even those who do not belong to the "sand-pile," are not only greatly interested, but decidedly more proud than envious of it. It seems remarkable that during all the years of its existence no boy has been mean enough to injure or plunder it at night, or angry enough to demolish anything of importance. This latter is of course in part due to the gradual habit of settling matters of dispute that are wont to be brought to an issue with fists and feet by meetings and speechifications. The accumulation of values here as elsewhere begets not only conservatism, but mutual forbearance and consideration. Most destructive in the "sand-pile" are little girls, who quite fail to appreciate it save in spots, as it were, and are therefore as far as possible excluded.

The institution is in general very real to the boys, though in different degrees to different boys, and some parts and some periods of it more so than others. Sometimes they are so in earnest they rise early to play before breakfast. They pour out grain for the cattle, and tip them up on their noses that they may eat, and then must clean up after them. The cattle "promise" the younger boys not to eat the beans, and the wooden figures never talk about the boys behind their backs, for "they told us so," said one. Of all the names in use in the "sand-pile" but one has been invented, all the rest having been copied from real persons about them. They are little troubled by incongruities of size. Some barns cover between one and two acres, and a horse could almost be ground up and put into a bushel measure, etc. Yet in a general way relative sizes are fairly preserved. It is a striking feature, to which I have observed no exception, that the more finished and like reality the objects became the less interest the boys had in them. As the tools, houses, etc., acquired feature after feature of verisimilitude, the sphere of the imagination was restricted as it is with too finished toys, and thus one of the chief charms of play was lost. Often the entire day was spent with almost no intermission in the business of the "sand-pile," and all went very pleasantly when perfect harmony

reigned. Most of the play-time of nearly every day of
the boys most interested for several summers has been
devoted to its very diversified direct and indirect interests.

As boys reach the age of fourteen, more or less, the
"sand-pile" gradually loses its charm, and seems childish
and unreal. One member of the circle was, I think, fifteen, and had become quite alive to its fictitious nature.
Unimaginative boys have proved mischievous and a
source of constant annoyance to those who took everything in dead earnest. Thus, it has been realized that to
admit aliens indiscriminately, or especially boys who had
begun to imagine themselves young gentlemen, was dangerous. Indeed, I fancy that the golden age of this ideal
little republic has already passed, and that a period of
over-refinement and ennervating luxury is likely, if it has
not done so with the close of the last summer, to end its
career. It was known that I was to visit it in the fall
again and perhaps write a brief sketch of it; it was
decked out to be photographed; the young lady with her
aesthetic paint-brush had introduced new ideals, for
paint decorates bad wood-work; the "sand-pile," being
near the roadside, attracted more and more notice. The
carpenter took to making miniature saws, saw-horses,
squares, screw-drivers, planes, vices, and other tools, copy-
ing his own tools for beauty more than for use, and, in
short, a gradual self-consciousness supervened, so that
the boys came to have in mind the applause of adult
spectators as well as their own pure interest. They have
long been wont to call themselves, in some relations to
their wooden figures, the *giants*—somewhat as their parents in a sense represent, when they have occasion, as is
most rare, to interfere, the blind fate that rules Jove
himself. I thought I observed that the giants were more
high-handed, and prone to intervene in the natural work-

ing out of problems and events, as a miracle-working Providence is sometimes said to break in on the order of nature. There seemed to be a slowly decreasing autonomy, heralding the decline of full-blooded boyishness and the far-away dawn of a new and reconstructed adolescent consciousness.

Still, when the inevitable return to Cambridge and school comes at last, the boys, it was said, seem for some time to be left with less eager interest in events, and to be some time in getting up as strong a zest for anything else. It is not that they become indifferent or pessimistic in the least degree, yet possibly life seems a little cheap and servile. They tried to colonize the "sand-pile" here, but Cambridge is too large to oversee and copy, and they were soon lost in trying to light their houses at night from within, and in constructing a system of drainage and sewerage, etc., and gave it up to spend play-time in the less absorbing ways of following and imitating the college ball games, and making houses, horses, and new inventions for next summer's "sand-pile."

On the whole, the "sand-pile" has, in the opinion of the parents, been of about as much yearly educational value to the boys as the eight months of school. Very many problems that puzzle older brains have been met in simpler terms and solved wisely and well. The spirit and habit of active and even prying observation has been greatly quickened. Industrial processes, institutions, and methods of administration and organization have been appropriated and put into practice. The boys have grown more companionable and rational, learned many a lesson of self-control, and developed a spirit of self-help. The parents have been enabled to control indirectly the associations of their boys, and, in a very mixed boy-community, to have them in a measure under obser-

vation without in the least restricting their freedom. The
habit of loafing and the evils that attend it has been
avoided, a strong practical and even industrial bent has
been given to their development, and much social morality has been taught in the often complicated *modus
vivendi* with others that has been evolved. Finally, this
may perhaps be called one illustration of the education
according to *nature* we so often hear and speak of. Each
element in this vast variety of interests is an organic part
of a comprehensive whole, compared with which the
concentrative methodic unities of Ziller seem artificial,
and, as Bacon said of scholastic methods, very inadequate
to subtility of nature. All the power of motive arising
from a large surface of interest is here turned on to the
smallest part. Had the elements of all the subjects involved in the "sand-pile," industrial, administrative,
moral, geographical, mathematical, etc., been taught sep-
arately and as mere school exercises, the result would
have been worry, waste, and chaos. Here is perfect mental sanity and unity, but with more variety than in the
most heterogeneous and soul-disintegrating school-cur-
riculum. The unity of all the diverse interests and activities of the "sand-pile" is, as it always is, ideal. There is
nothing so practical in education as the ideal, nor so ideal
as the practical. This means not less that brain-work and
hand-work should go together than that the general and
special must help each other in order to produce the best
results. As boys are quickened by the imagination to
realize their conceptions of adult life, so men are best
stimulated to greatest efforts by striving to realize the
highest human ideals, whether those actualized in the
lives of the best men, the best pages of history, or the
highest legitimate, though yet unrealized, ideals of tradition and the future.

4. Children's Collections*

The following brief report illustrates Hall's approach to child study. Typically, he selected a general pattern of behavior, in this instance, children collecting objects, and recruited an enthusiastic disciple to gather data. Hall's conviction that child study should be useful is illustrated by the bits of advice given for handling the "collecting instinct" in the school.

Miss Sara E. Wiltse, who has been for several years a systematic observer of childhood, sent to the writer some time ago along with a mass of other valuable but as yet undigested material, the answers of 227 Boston school-boys of fifteen and sixteen years of age, to a short set of questions about their collections. Of this number only nineteen had never made collections they deemed worth reporting. One hundred and forty-four reported collections of two kinds of objects; ninety-five of three kinds; twenty-eight of four kinds, and a few of five and more kinds. Stamps were most frequently collected; then followed in order of frequency, coins; marbles, sometimes to the number of several thousand; advertising or business cards; pictures; stones, ores, minerals, and sometimes even bits of brick and chalk; woods, leaves or flowers, insects, eggs, shells; scrap-books of all sorts (generally funny stories), imprints of the die of local

* *The Pedagogical Seminary,* I (June, 1891), 234–237.

post-offices, riddles, autographs; buttons, nut-galls, bird's nests, smooth or colored stones, and even toadstools, peachstones, lists of names, tools and many other things. Of the three most common collections, that of marbles nearly always comes first, and begins, on the average, very soon after the beginning of public school life, and lasts from three to six years. The passion for stamps comes later, and coins later yet; the average interval between the latter, as well as their duration, cannot be inferred from the data. These collections have been made quite independently of school work, and, so far as can be inferred from the writing, spelling and syntax of the written returns, the brightest boys have made most collections, and in each of these respects the nineteen boys who have no collections to report are below the average, though by no means always the worst.

Several observers have sent in returns from school-girls of equal age to similar questions, but as yet the returns are too few and too imperfect to have much statistical value. It appears, however, that the passion for collections is less strong in girls, and the objects most often collected are different. Little girls often collect bows from adults, keeping tally on bits of paper, and older girls collect flowers, cloth and paper patterns, bric-a-brac, keepsakes, etc., as well as in many cases making the same collections as the boys. It is evident that more data are wanted for both sexes before the effect of age, temperament, locality, conditions of life, sex, etc., can be determined, and it is to be hoped that teachers or superintendents who have superior facilities will address themselves to further studies of this important topic.

It seems already plain, however, that this instinct is a strong and almost universal force in human nature, which the school should study and use more than it does.

It is one of the chief juvenile expressions of the instinct on which the induction and specialization of natural sciences rests. Museums of all sorts and sizes, literary collections, and even the gathering of the above data about this instinct rest upon it. In fact, almost any and every interest may prompt collections, and be made the nucleus of scientific culture sometimes for the very boys who get least from the ordinary school. There might easily be in most country towns, if not in each school building, small working collections, made largely by the children themselves, illustrating local geology, woods, plants, birds and animals, mounted or put up in the most educational way, and, with a few pictured books, made the basis of general or class exercises. This, we believe, may at least be suggestive in solving the great question how more and better natural science may be taught in schools of the lower grades. Teachers of literature, also, even in lower grammar-school grades, have induced their pupils to gather from many sources, by scrap-books and otherwise, literary specimens which especially interested them, and thus, as it were, to make individual reading-books—their own in a sense which is of great educational significance.

But if data like the above show the force, they do not suggest the danger attending this passion, viz: that it degenerates toward the blind mania for collecting objects *(Sammeltrieb)* seen in certain forms of mental disease, and even in some species of animals. Our returns show scores of boys who collect stamps or coins with very little of the knowledge of the geography and history needful to give a rational interest to their collections; who gather blindly and mechanically large numbers of eggs with no knowledge of the species, or merely the tails of birds or squirrels, with not only no knowledge of their characteristics or manner of mounting, but without even the most common hunter's knowledge of their habits. When we reflect how much might be taught incidentally by the rapid way of suggestion, if given while these interests were at their hottest, and put tactfully, perhaps in the form of directions for improving collections already begun, we can realize how considerable is the educational loss. And yet correctives are not so easily made effective as would at first seem. Collections do not always imply the knowledge or even the high degree of mental curiosity they are wont to suggest. Museum values and scientific values are often divergent, and may be almost opposite. Much might be written of the cases in which undue haste to catalogue or to collect had robbed objects of scientific worth. How often, again, do we see in our laboratories even advanced students making and mounting histologic sections day after day, to get good collections of slides, in a thoughtless and mechanical way, or even in original research repeating observations and enlarging protocols without so carrying everything in mind that each product is subjected to the highest degree of scrutiny it is capable of as they go along, and thus lose time under the illusion that they are doing real scientific work. It is such hard work to think, and there are so many proxies and simulacra of thought that deceive even well-trained men—it is so much easier to get ready to think, as the miser hoards in order to get ready to live —that the way of true science is indeed straight and narrow.

All this, nevertheless, does not make us for a moment doubt that this is an educable instinct, and that it has head enough, wherever it is wisely turned on to school mechanism, to quicken especially all those elements of school work that are associated with Comenius, Locke, object-lessons and science-teaching. It is not ready-made, purchased, but individual collections, with the sense of personal ownership on the part of those who made them in no wise relaxed, but used in a way to make the school-house interesting, because reflecting at the same time the local characteristics and local pride, that we need.* How each of the above kinds of collections and others can be best utilized in or by the school, is a problem which only the experience of the practical teacher can solve; and when it and the other unfinished questions above suggested are determined, it will make, if we are not mistaken, a valuable as well as for the most part a new chapter in pedagogy.

* Hall's Teutonic syntax might best be rendered as follows: It is not ready-made, purchased collections that we need, but individual collections, with the sense of personal ownership on the part of those who made them in no wise relaxed, but used in a way to make the school-house interesting, because reflecting at the same time local characteristics and local pride.—C. E. S. and C. B.

5. Child-Study and Its Relation to Education*

At the height of the enthusiasm for child study, Hall undertook a lengthy explanation and defense of the movement it had generated. Although acknowledging its weaknesses, he insisted on the value of the endeavor for a science of psychology and for an education respectful of the "true nature and needs of childhood." The following article also anticipated Hall's subsequent emphasis on adolescence as a critical stage in human development.

Child-study or paidology, often confused with psychogenesis, of which it constitutes a large part, is a new movement which has been well under way hardly a decade. It is already represented by a bibliography of some two thousand titles, including only the books and articles well worth reading, and not comprising the yet larger mass of chaff; by two journals in this country devoted exclusively to it, and by several more which make it a department; by three journals in Germany, two in France, one each in England, Italy, Japan, Russia, and Spain.

Paidology either forms a department, or appears on the programme of most of the leading psychological, philosophical, and educational societies. Its work is supported from the treasury of several of the largest States.

* *The Forum,* XXIX (August, 1900), 688–693, 696–702.

Sometimes, as, for example, in New York city, it is a topic in the annual school reports; and expert investigations are paid for out of the municipal treasury. There are several academic chairs devoted mainly or exclusively to it; and I opine that it enters somewhat into the instruction of nearly every course of study that deals with the human mind. There are organizations with which I have been in correspondence in India, South America, Russia, Spain, and Australia; and circles or groups exist in almost every civilized or colonized land.

Studies of child life among the North American Indians, Australian tribes, the Zulus, Chinese, clay-eaters, Kaffirs, Maoris, Arabs, Samoyads, ancient Greeks and Romans, etc., are found in periodicals or publishers' announcements. Child-study forms a section or a part of the work of nearly all the leading women's clubs, summer schools, and organizations of Sunday-school teachers. It is a movement that has been extensively felt in literature, as witness the many books on childhood noticed during the last few years in the journals I edit; and it is even a frequent topic in the daily, weekly, and, especially, the Sunday newspaper press. Teachers of all grades, mothers of all degrees of culture, pupils in colleges and normal schools fill out questionnaires, and perhaps meet to compare results and to report the latest magazine literature upon the subject. I have received some two thousand letters—either unacknowledged or inadequately answered—from all parts of the world, asking how to organize local work, requesting suggestions for reading, or very often seeking advice concerning children. A private secretary devoted solely to this work could do beneficent service; and perhaps a new profession might arise, which might be indicated by some such term as psychic orthopedics or pediatrics.

The teachers foremost in the work are usually the best among the younger men and women, and the academic representation is naturally strongest among those who have not developed the conservatism of age. This, of course, is auspicious, because the ideals of young men and women are proverbially the best material for prophecy. It is obvious that there is often enthusiasm without knowledge, and also that there are a great many camp followers and faddists in the child-study movement, such as are to be found in the wake of all movements when they assume certain proportions. On the other hand, while the work has had plenty of attacks, often bitter and virulent, it has so far had no competent criticism. Like a new planet, it has disturbed the circles of the systematizers, who live and move in the sphere of definitions, and lay down the law for sciences new and old, like surveyors plotting imaginary streets, or policemen enforcing city rules in the country. But critics such as these have so far uniformly violated Coleridge's sensible adage, that we should see to it that we are not ignorant of an author's understanding before we attempt to understand his ignorance. The defenders of things as they are and the leaders of the rear guard of conservatism, who a few years ago poured out their vials of wrath and contempt, are already in various stages of compromise and adjustment.

It is a nondescript and, in some sense, an unparalleled movement—partly psychology, partly anthropology, partly medico-hygiene. It is closely related at every step to the study of instinct in animals, and to the rites and beliefs of primitive people; and it has a distinct ethico-philosophical aspect—partly what a recent writer classed as the higher biology—with a spice of folk-lore and of religious evolution, sometimes with an alloy of gossip and nursery tradition, but possessing a broad, practical side in the pedagogy of all stages. It has all the advantages and the less grave disadvantages of its many-sidedness.

The point of view of the pedagogue, and also of the psychologist, is like that of the one-ninth of an iceberg visible above water, and each often marvels, especially if hostile, that it goes nearly as well straight in the teeth of his disfavor and indifferently with or against the wind of his approval, because he does not see the submerged eight-ninths of it controlled by the currents of a denser medium. An able classifier and over-systematizer deplores that pedagogy "wants to marry psychology." He is belated; they were made one years ago. The physician, who weighs and measures, tests eyes, ears, etc., is hardly in sight of the philologist, who studies the development of language in the child's speech; and neither knows nor cares much for the unfoldment of the child's sense of self, fear, anger, superstition, nascent periods of interest, capacity, etc.

The uniqueness of the situation consists thus in the new direction and focalization of many scientific departments and methods upon one object, some of which have never before had even this bond of union. Again, the coöperation of the eminent professorial expert with the utterly untrained parent or primary teacher—so that each has an interest in the same matter, and the former awaits the latter's publication with both a filial and a proprietary interest—is a novelty shocking to the esoteric instincts traditional in academic life. It is not strange, therefore, if excessive hopes and fears have been aroused.

One of the oldest objections against child-study, now very rarely heard, is that it is liable to interfere in some way with the naïveté of children, and to make them self-conscious. A few years ago I heard a prominent professor declare, with great emphasis, before an audience of applauding Boston school-masters, that, as for his own children, they should never be mentally vivisected; that they should be loved, not studied, etc. "All that I have to say out of my deepest heart is, simply, I do not believe in it." A prominent New York daily about that time, with most sensational headlines, accused a leading professor of Columbia of subjecting his own children to research, as if it were a new and diabolical species of torture. I lately saw in a yellow journal of Chicago an illustrated account of a Normal School girl who wanted to fill out a questionnaire on crying, and who, after waiting in vain for a fortnight, until her composition was due, actually pinched her baby brother's ear to get material.

I am ready to take this in all seriousness, and say candidly that if such studies injure ever so little the very few observed for the benefit of the very many we have no adequate warrant for this work. However precious the scientific results, they would be bought at too dear a price. Better a millstone about our necks, and we in the sea, than that we offend the little ones in this way. But the truth is the exact opposite. The best data are gathered as one of the offices of love, with a view to making the tender influences of parents or of school, or of both, more effective; and I cannot think that instincts generally so true are here perverted.

Love and study in this field, as in that of natural science, instead of interfering with, strengthen each other. Not only are we better parents and teachers for both knowing and doing this work, but those who fail to utilize it are neglecting some of the most urgent new duties of a new age. I have received hundreds of letters from parents, who, for the most part, express gratitude that they have learned from it things of vital importance for the welfare of their children; and I could spend much of my time in testing psychical qualities and applying results for parents who write to me or call on me for help about their children. I cannot believe that all these people have perverted instincts in wanting their children investigated, or that those who express gratitude do so because the mind is enlightened, or seeks to become so, at the expense of the heart.

I have selected fifty topics which seem to me as valuable and representative as any; and in only one of these can there be any question concerning injury or inconvenience in the work of collecting data. There have been studies of very delicate questions; but I know of no case where, even in such instances, precautions were not taken that would satisfy a critic, even if he were constitutionally sentimental or disposed to be sensational.

In the majority of my fifty topics the children never suspect, from first to last, that they are being observed at all, as, *e.g.,* in plays and games, signs of fatigue, automatic movements, positions of the hand, cases of imitation, infant's creeping. In other cases they tap, press a dynamometer, count lines, put a needle through a small hole, read different types a few minutes, name their favorite story, are tested for defects of the eye, ear, power of speech, are weighed, measured, etc. In other topics, like fear, the very calling of attention to these psychoses, which have often secretly haunted adolescence for years, has, in itself, helped toward their dissipation and control, and aided pitiable cases toward what Aristotle said is the definition of education itself—"Learning to fear aright."

What more pathetic object in the world can there be than a misunderstood child? As the elective system is working its way down toward high, and even grammar, school grades, it becomes more important to fit it to the nature and needs of individual children, in order that the school may become a life-and-career-saving institution. Very strange to say, only those whose philosophy is ultra-introspective fear self-consciousness or interference with the naturalness of children. Self-knowledge is a very different thing from self-consciousness; and it is only from the former standpoint that the highest study of mankind is man, and that next to the highest is childhood. There is here a new duty, which is neglected by parents who do not love their children intelligently enough to study them.

Again, some critics have objected to this part of the work—that matter collected by untrained observers can have no value. They ignore, however, the obvious difference between the gathering of raw material and the manufacture of it into forms of value, processes as distinct as the work of the quarryman and the sculptor. Almost any intelligent mother can tell me whether her child has a passion for collecting buttons, bottles, or postage stamps; whether it is attended by imaginary companions; what kind of dolls it plays with; when it cut its first teeth; what mistakes it makes most frequently in addition; what diseases it has had; what are its favorite toys and games. The more skilful can collect data on intense and chronic fears, on manifestations of anger, imitations, automatisms, excessive blushing, number forms; can measure or weigh; can answer a few questions on laughing and crying, creeping, the senses, motor power, only children, the development of language, and many other topics.

The four largest anthropological societies—those of England, France, Germany, and Italy—have each issued little hand-books directing untrained observers who may happen to be among savage races how to collect more complicated data than these, including even vocabularies, religious rites and ideas, and social institutions; and the savants make large use of returns from such sources. A little practice with such material, aided by some experience in collecting data upon the subject, enables the expert frequently to master the sometimes rather difficult problem of the sources of error, to weed it out, boil data down, and in some cases transform it as much as the watch-spring maker metamorphoses the crude ore of the miner into products of a very high value.

It may be somewhat as the physician consults the mother about his patient, or the judge questions an unlettered witness. In general, however, the critics do those who make returns great injustice and dispraise. Among some scores of thousands of returns which I have dealt with, directly or indirectly, many are from leading college professors, more from college graduates, and very many from students. From considerable practice others have developed very rare skill in getting valuable data from their students. No one can begin to appreciate the difficulties in this field or the methods by which they are successfully overcome who has not himself had considerable experience with the work. It is an expert problem, in which the opinions of experts only have value.

Mixed in with the best, there is, indeed, material that is more chaffy than any antagonist I know of has sampled. Perhaps I go too far in holding that, where the quality of work in a great and new field, like this, ranges all the way from utter worthlessness to the very highest value, a critic with real magnanimity would select the best; but I maintain that not only the animus, but also the ability, of a critic is indicated by the grade of work he attacks. Here any one can vanquish to absurdity the weaklings, but no one can impugn the best. I sympathize somewhat with the abler critics in such success as they achieve in the modest task of showing up sub-average work. Like the reformation, or evolution itself, although as yet not comparable in depth and breadth with these great culture movements, genetic psychology has taken a strong hold upon the popular mind, and has enlisted a crowd of camp-followers—some for profit and repute, as the movement gathers breadth and momentum, and others, utterly untrained, whose enthusiasm prompts them to attempt things beyond their power. On the whole I have felt hitherto that perhaps the wheat and tares might best grow together a while longer, lest modest merit be discouraged; and I even fail to see why it is more absurd to show a baby to a class in psychology than to one of medical students, if the conditions chance to favor.

·   ·   ·

Much is written about the methods as if they were rivals. This can never be, for all methods are good. Some, like Preyer, Shinn, Moore, and Baldwin, prefer to focus their work upon one or two children, and to bring to this focus the best they can from the anthropometric, physiological, philological, psychological, and, perhaps, other fields. This is as legitimate as it is to study plants or animals from the standpoint of chemistry, biology, physics, etc.; but experts excel in only one or two lines, and the monographs under this class have their weak as well as their strong points. Moreover, one must adhere very closely to a plain and painstaking record of facts here; hoping that, through the accumulation of a vast body of data, inferences of value may some time be drawn.

One of the above-mentioned authors may perhaps come to stand as a striking illustration of the danger of drawing general conclusions and building speculative conclusions upon a monopaidic basis. We have several interesting memoirs devoted to the very detailed and monographic study of a single case of some typical form of insanity; and the very elaborate application of the method of many sciences to the study of Zola's personality, which lately appeared, suggests a new factor in biographic work. The work done on Casper Hauser, Laura Bridgeman, and the Juke family, illustrates the method.

Another method is to select a single topic or question, and gather data upon it from many children. This, obviously, affords the expert—whether he be a student of language, of the eye or ear, of psychology or pedagogy—a chance to focus more sharply upon one special subject, of scores of which every child is a collection. Some, like Barnes, Boaz, Bowditch, do their best work here by gathering data from very large numbers; others limit themselves to one or a few dozen for more careful work, like Ament, Starbuck, etc. Some, like Miss Williams, Wiltse, Small, etc., do best by gathering material for the express purpose of one topic; while others, led by Principal Russell, collect salient facts of all sorts and let them naturally group themselves about topics later.

Here, perhaps, I might instance my own studies of fears, anger, dolls, laughing and crying, a sense of self, children's collections, contents of their minds on entering school, etc. The object here is to make what Bacon would call a *silva silvarium,* or a large collection of actual

facts, and later to group them according to sex, age, etc.,
so as to present something a little like a composite photo-
graph of the subject. Each individual life is in most
respects so limited in its experience that the enlargement
of these themes by the comparative method brings out
many new and unsuspected features, and is remotely
analogous to the use of the microscope.

The simple reading of a copious anthology of well-
made and sifted records is for me not only most interesting, but among the most instructive of all forms of
psychological literature. It brings one in contact with life
on a larger scale; brings out in strong colors what was
latent in individual experience; and enriches and ampli-
fies one's knowledge of human nature. I do not wonder
that in some normal schools and colleges these bare data,
properly grouped and ordered, take the place of text-book
instruction. They resemble the physician's personal acquaintance with a rich casuistic material in a hospital of
general cases.

Upon the value of the genetic movement for psychology I shall not dwell here, but shall pass to the much-
discussed question of its utility for teachers. If psychology be conceived epistemologically as dealing with inner
facts primarily non-spacial—that can never be communi-
cated, described, or measured, that have meaning and
value only when transformed according to logical ideals
which seek an expression of reality sharply demarcated
with water-tight compartments from art, history, physiology, and life itself, so that it might almost be called a psychology devitalized, or versus life—then every teacher in
the land may well breathe a sigh of relief to be told that
his work is strictly anti-psychological, and that he has not
the slightest use for this science.

This utter divorce is, if possible, still further justified

if teaching be conceived solely as instruction, or the lodgment of knowledge in mental receptacles, with no reference to methods, or to the predispositions, interests, capacities, etc., of the pupil. However much this may violate the oldest and perhaps most cherished American tradition, that the mental and moral sciences must define the goal and carefully work out the methods of both textbooks and class work, we must submit as victims of these new and jejune definitions that triangulate so many vast mental spaces.

From such conceptions, however valuable in their abstract sphere, I believe all healthful psychological thinking revolts. For one, my conception of psychology is as different from all this as science is from epistemology or metaphysics. I propound here no definitions, but urge that we must, in justice to the human soul, conceive it far more broadly and vitally. From one view-point it is the natural history of the human and prehuman mind in all its aspects, from the ant, bee and wasp up. I would not exclude it from any phenomena of life to which we can apply the term selection.

The psychologist should be in love with life, especially human life, in every aspect of it, as broadly as the author of the *Comédie Humaine* conceived his theme. He passionately loves the acquaintance and friendship of animals, would know their ways, and divine, if he could, how the world looks beneath the skull of the beaver, the dog, or the chimpanzee. He frequents institutions for defectives—the blind, deaf, idiots, insane—where nature has made her great, but cruel, experiments. He loves and is at home with children; is on as familiar terms as is practicable with savages and criminals; frequents the psychological laboratory; and is versed in the history of the great systems. He is penetrated with the faith that even the latter may, and sometime will, be explained in the larger evolutionary way as we explain migrations, nest-building, and the social organization of animals. This is plain, naturalistic thinking, with a standpoint as objective as that of the sciences, but including every addition that self-observation and introspection can make, recognizing, of course, the peculiar conditions that must prevail here.

From this standpoint it is plain that the teacher must know two things: (1) the subject matter to be taught; and (2) the nature and capacity of the minds in which it is to be rooted. The farmer must know soils as well as seeds; the architect, the nature of material as well as ground-plans and elevations; the physician, his patient's history, and perhaps that of his family, and he must know drugs as well—all partial, but helpful, analogies. If logic and the old philosophy of mind have ever helped the teacher, the new genetic conceptions are incalculably more labor-saving in his work.

Let us consider a single representative point. Every one recognizes the importance of interest, how it quickens attention, short-circuits slower processes, and eases the strain of acquisition, and how the teacher who is well informed on the favorite out-of-school amusements and occupations of his pupils, and on the life led by them, and who knows his classes individually and collectively, can shorten the road of learning. To determine and group these interests more fully than ever occurred to Herbart is one of the quests of child-study. One of its goals now near at hand, and which will involve considerable change both in regard to the methods of teaching every subject in the curriculum and the age at which the different subjects can be most profitably taught, is the determination of nascent periods for both mental and muscular work. We shall very soon have curves of the years when many of the chief culture-interests begin to culminate and decline. This will enable us to say definitely which are the premature and which are the belated subjects; *i.e.*, when the matter of school training can be taught without forcing, and without sinning away the sacred hour of maximal receptivity and capacity.

Among the more incidental advantages of the study of children is the new bond which it often establishes between the home and the school. The teacher who no longer regards his pupils as marionettes, to be treated as groups or classes, but as free units, with a bond of sympathy between each of their hearts and his own, desires to know at least something of the home life of each child, and to come to an understanding with parents. Hence, many very different organizations have arisen, from Superintendent Dutton's educational club in Brookline, Massachusetts, to the circles of mothers who meet the teachers weekly after school at Detroit, Michigan. Again, women teachers are increasing, and the method by which they do their best work is to consider individuals and adapt themselves to personal differences. Child study gives sanction to this method, reinforces it, and tends to make the teacher's service of even greater pecuniary value.

Another advantage of interest in child-study is that it helps to break down to some extent the partitions between grades of work, so that the kindergartner and university professor can coöperate in the same task. Best of all, perhaps, it tends to make family life with plenty of children in it more interesting and desirable. Indeed, it is a part of a great culture-movement marked by a new love of the naïve, the spontaneous, and the unsophisticated, by a desire to get at what is primitive and original in human nature as it comes fresh from its primal sources. A prevalent theory of art insists that the greatest defect of all art-products is a sign of conscious design, and that the acme of aesthetic enjoyment is reached when it is realized that the poem or picture is a product of unconscious creative force more or less irresistible, and, as with the greatest geniuses, with no thought of effect. Just so in childhood we are coming again to realize that in its fresh thoughts, feelings, and impulses, we have an oracle which declares that the world and human nature are sound to the core.

More yet. There is really no clue by which we can thread our way through all the mazes of culture and the distractions of modern life save by knowing the true nature and needs of childhood and of adolescence. I urge, then, that civilizations, religions, all human institutions, and the schools, are judged truly, or from the standpoint of the philosophy of history, by this one criterion: namely, whether they have offended against these little ones or have helped to bring childhood and adolescence to an ever higher and completer maturity as generations pass by. Childhood is thus our pillar of cloud by day and fire by night. Other oracles may grow dim, but this one will never fail.

Just as at various times in the history of culture man has turned with renewed zest to the old and ultimate humanistic question of what he really is, his place and meaning in the universe, his whence and whither, so now we are asking with unique interest what a child really is. We are slowly awakening to a recognition that children are not like adults, with all the faculties of maturity on a reduced scale, but unique and very different creatures. Their proportions are so different that if head, body, and limbs were each to grow in its original proportion until they reached adult stature, they would be monsters. Adaptable as children are, their ways and thoughts are not as ours; and the adult can no more get back into the child's soul by introspection than he can pass the flaming sword and reclaim his lost Eden. The recollections of our own childhood are the mere flotsam and jetsam of a wrecked stage of development; and the lost points in psychogenesis must be slowly wrought out with toil and patience.

The child's senses, instincts, views of truth, credulity, emotions, and feelings toward objects have very little in common with ours, and indeed are sometimes almost incommensurate; so that we have to explore our way back slowly and tediously, with many an indirect method, if we would solve the great problem that looms before us. The study of a few hundred biographies of great men reveals a large floating body of storiology that is liable to attach itself to the early years of any one who afterwards attains eminence. This has shown that most of the material constituting the records of childhood and even adolescence is nearly as mythic as Niebuhr found the stories of early Roman history to be. This, although perhaps the very least of all the motivations to it, suggests the advisability of a life and health book as one of the inalienable rights of childhood, which children would be the first to claim if they knew enough to make a declaration of their rights.

In some European towns such books are now opened by municipal order, and are kept through required school life. Here all the monthly examinations through all the years are a standing witness of the child's progress and fitness for advancement. The school doctor here records his fears and advice, the parents perhaps add their comments, and, in rare cases, the anthropologist or special student supplements all this; so that on the whole there could hardly be a more useful document for giving each child a serviceable kind of self-knowledge of his own strong and weak points as an aid in the choice of a vocation.

One of the most important themes, both practically and scientifically, is adolescence, the springtime of life, when the emotional nature undergoes nothing less than a regeneration, when the child normally passes from egoism to altruism, and the great subordination of the individual to the race slowly makes itself manifest. This is the most critical period of life, because civilization depends on whether these uncertain final stages, which most differentiate man from animals, shall be completed or arrested. When the nature of this period is understood, and its needs are met, the most radical of all educational changes will be found necessary in the high school and early collegiate years in ways I have elsewhere indicated. Every race, savage and enlightened, has recognized this stage. Indeed, in a sense, education begins here, and widens upward to the university and downward toward the kindergarten, somewhat in proportion as civilization advances.

Regarded from the standpoint of the highest biologic law this adolescent stage is the golden period of life. The faculties of both body and soul here reach their acme. Just as the ape reaches at adolescence that point in his development which is nearest to man, and becomes farther from him as he matures, so the human race grows younger and more adolescent, because at this stage only the bud of the super-man that is to be appears.

III

The Child-Centered School

". . . there is nothing else so worthy of love, reverence, and service as the body and soul of the growing child."

6.   New Departures in Education*

*While still a professor at Johns Hopkins, Hall sided with
the forces demanding a "new" education. A popular
article, part of which is reprinted here, expressed his
conviction that the common school lacked a true reverence for the nature of childhood and was blind to the
critical role education could play in shaping the future
of civilization.*

If quantity and mechanism are the standards of merit
in education, our country excels all others. The American child uses three or four times as many pages of
text-books in a year as the European child. In the average
excellence of our school-buildings; in the remarkable
order and discipline of our school-rooms; in the consummate perfection of our marking systems, by which not
only the lesson-getting but often the conduct of the
largest classes is graded on a scale so fine and long that no
two pupils are alike; in the size of our educational meetings and number of papers read; in the number of our
educational journals, now over sixty; in the number of
educational publishing houses and the bulk of their
productions; in these respects Columbia beats all creation. "At this moment," said the superintendent of
schools in a certain large city, taking out his watch, "so
many thousand children here are reciting their grammar

* *The North American Review,* CXL (February, 1885), 144–147.

lesson, and in so many minutes they will all turn to arithmetic." A Sunday-school authority lately declared that as the sun moved across our land, one day in every seven, about seven million children and adults, with little distinction of age or method, would be "on Abraham's sacrifice." Growth in bigness of these many sorts, with statistical illustrations, is the theme of many school reports, addresses, etc., and horizontal expansion has its inspirations. Although, compared with other lands, we almost never have the best in education, we rarely have the worst. But the very vastness, uniformity, and average mechanical excellence of our school system as a whole, admirable as it is in itself, and indispensable as it is for all higher developments, make it less plastic than it should be to the rapidly deepening apprehensions of the very complex conditions of setting children to learn what humanity has toiled to discover and striven to do and be in the world. Our printed courses of study, often so detailed and exiguous* as to destroy all the teacher's freedom and initiative, and our examination papers and exhibitions, which too often more than make up for lack of thoroughness by the number of studies begun, show off the children so well that we forget that many of our schools are, as has been said, working out here the problem that China has solved so well, viz., how to instruct and not develop. Worst of all is the attempt of the so-called philosophy of this mechanism to meet the rising demand that the school shall do something for morals, by so distinguishing between the functions of church, state, family, and school, that only the above-named methods seem proper for the latter; when the fact is, the only thing that can ever undermine our school system in

* Hall evidently meant "exigent," that is, exacting.—C. E. S. and C. B.

popular support is a suspicion that it does not moralize as well as mentalize children. This antiquated philosophy of education has no open questions, except into which pigeon-hole, in a predetermined system, new facts and ideas shall go; and it quite forgets that rudiments of the studies are not first principles (at least save in exact sciences, and rarely there), and that the logical order in which subjects are best apprehended by the adult or scientific mind is very different from, and often inconsistent with, the arts of adaptation. This is what we now mean by the "old" in education. It has done great things for us in the past, and is an indispensable basis for future progress. Its danger is complacency and routine; and when we reflect on the sad fatality by which everything in education always tends to gravitate toward the worst, without great and unremitting effort and enthusiasm,—a worst that involves national decay and even calamity,— it may be well to ask ourselves whether such a system is not, on the whole, better adapted to educate henchmen of political and other bosses, civil and religious, than freemen, and to enfeeble moral and muscular fiber, and breed actual distrust for books and mental culture by cram.

The new education, on the other hand (if we may venture to indicate roughly the ever-shifting line between the old and the new in this field), holds that there is one thing in nature, and one alone, fit to inspire all true men and women with more awe and reverence than Kant's starry heavens, and that is the soul and the body of the healthy young child. Heredity has freighted it with all the accumulated results of parental well and ill doing, and filled it with reverberations from a past more vast than science can explore; and on its right development depends the entire future of civilization two or three decades hence. Simple as childhood seems, there is nothing harder to know; and responsive as it is to every influence about it, nothing is harder to guide. To develop childhood to virtue, power, and due freedom is the supreme end of education, to which everything else should be subordinated as means. Just as to command inanimate nature we must constantly study, love, obey her, so to control child nature we must first, and perhaps still more piously, study, love, obey it. The best of us teachers have far more to learn from children than we can ever hope to teach them; and what we succeed in teaching, at least beyond the merest rudiments, will always be proportionate to the knowledge we have the wit to get from and about them.

Every important advance or reform in the history of education has been in large measure due to new insights into the nature of childhood, dispelling the mazes of error that are spun with such strange persistence and abundance through the minds of adults about it. There is a partition that insensibly rises between the adult and the child, as between the educated and the uneducated mind, which must be laboriously broken down. Pestalozzi dressed, washed, combed, aired, and slept in the midst of his pauper school-children, shared all their joys and sorrows, and effected his reforms because he had at last come to live in their world, and learned and told something new of childhood. Locke, Froebel, Herbart, Hamilton, Bell, Lancaster, Stowe, Wilderspen, Necker, and most of the teachers whose work and words it is worth our while to ponder in the history of education, studied children, often in a systematic way, as a naturalist studies the instincts of insects and animals; and their exhortation is to follow, observe, adapt to the nature of childhood. Knowledge of the subject to be taught, though so commonly defective, is only the beginning of the teacher's wisdom, especially in all primary and intermediate education. He must look solely at the pupil, and sacrifice, if need be, any method or logical order to the law of exigency, which requires instruction to be given whenever, wherever, and however interest is hottest and curiosity most alert. Premature, belated, ill-adapted information, given without determining just how much knowledge can be presupposed as the point of departure, this is the cram that makes bad, collapsible mental tissue, because not thoroughly digested and assimilated, and originates that worst product of artificial methods, a dislike of study and knowledge. All possible, or at least all common errors liable to arise in childish minds at each point of each study, or the great source of ignorance as it may be called, should be carefully studied. To secure some practical knowledge of this kind of juvenile psychology, which should determine the matter as well as the method of teaching, is the object of the graduate courses in pedagogy, or of the almost gratuitous year of probationary apprenticeship now required in several European countries before even the best scholars are allowed to teach. It also explains the partial truth of the monitorial system, that those could teach a subject best who had just learned it, and who also knew the style and language of the learners.

The new education of to-day looks at quality rather than quantity, and has chiefly in view two things: first, methods that are natural, and secondly, educational values—the highest of all kinds of value in the world. When we speak of truth for its own sake, apart from all utilities, we mean its purely educational value. In this sense it is well said that all sciences, religions, states, etc., exist and are good only because and in so far as they de-

velop man. It is plain that the wisest of the founders of
our political institutions realized far more than most of
us do, that in a country so free and so new, and without
authority, precedent, or tradition, only intelligence could
control the conditions of human development. Narrow
as their views of education were, they felt that in a peculiar sense it must be no less fundamental in a republic
like ours than in Plato's, where all problems were ultimately educational ones. The chief specialty of our
country must be education, if she is to maintain her
place among the powers of the civilized world. Here the
wisdom of true statesmanship must culminate. The law-
givers that will rule our land in the next century should
and must study well the problems of education. Scientifically, too, the next problem is, undoubtedly, man and
his faculties, first to know and then to control the conditions of his development—a most important aspect of
the whole problem. The question how high a development man can reach, the fundamental question of
civilizations, is likely, or at least ought, to be solved more
consciously, and with more design and intelligence here
than elsewhere; and hence, too, the great and peculiar
significance of our very few educational institutions of
highest rank.

·   ·   ·

7.   Childhood and Adolescence*

As Hall's own version of the child-centered school gradually emerged, it was influenced by his shift of interest from childhood to adolescence, a shift reinforced by his belief that youthful idealism is the key to social reform along the lines of evolutionary progress. Hall's first major work, a two-volume compilation of fact and opinion about adolescence, indicated clearly the direction of his thought. In the preface to that study, a portion of which is reprinted here, he attempted to relate psychology to education and social reform, at the same time formulating a developmental concept of childhood and adolescence, which proved to be the most characteristic of his doctrines. For Hall, the theory of recapitulation explained the striking contrast between the "savage" child and the "civilized" adolescent and suggested that the high school should be the focus of the "new" education.

Holding that the child and the race are each keys to the other, I have constantly suggested phyletic explanations of all degrees of probability. Some of these, I think, have been demonstrated so far as is now possible in this obscure and complicated domain. Realizing the limitations and qualifications of the recapitulation theory in the biologic field, I am now convinced that its psycho-

---

* *Adolescence* (New York: D. Appleton and Co., 1904), I, viii–xix.

genetic applications have a method of their own, and although the time has not yet come when any formulation of these can have much value, I have done the best I could with each instance as it arose. Along with the sense of the immense importance of further coordinating childhood and youth with the development of the race, has grown the conviction that only here can we hope to find true norms against the tendencies to precocity in home, school, church, and civilization generally, and also to establish criteria by which to both diagnose and measure arrest and retardation in the individual and the race. While individuals differ widely in not only the age but the sequence of the stages of repetition of racial history, a knowledge of nascent stages and the aggregate interests of different ages of life is the best safeguard against very many of the prevalent errors of education and of life.

Modern conceptions, which increasingly make all mental processes efferent in their psychophysical nature, suggest a now impending synthesis that may give to our practical age and land the long-hoped-for and long-delayed science of man. To help bring these tendencies to their maturity is the task to which organic thinkers should address themselves. Utilizing to the utmost the lessons of the past, they should free themselves alike from excessive subjectivisms and from the limitations of old systems and methods, and feel it their highest duty to enter upon the less critical and more constructive work of building larger philosophic mansions for the soul. If truth is edification, the highest criterion of pure science is its educative value. The largest possible aspect of all the facts of life and mind is educational, and the only complete history is the story of the influences that have advanced or retarded the development of man toward his completion, always ideal and forever in the future. Thus psychology and the higher pedagogy are one and inseparable. Not only the beautiful and the good, but the true, can have no other test of validity than that they appeal to and satisfy certain deep needs; and these are many. From this general view-point I have tried to show how truth about things of the soul, in an unique sense, is never complete or certain till it has been applied to education, and that the latter field is itself preeminent and unlike all other fields of application for either scientific or philosophic conclusions.

The years from about eight to twelve constitute an unique period of human life. The acute stage of teething is passing, the brain has acquired nearly its adult size and weight, health is almost at its best, activity is greater, and more varied than ever before or than it ever will be again, and there is peculiar endurance, vitality, and resistance to fatigue. The child develops a life of its own outside the home circle, and its natural interests are never so independent of adult influence. Perception is very acute, and there is great immunity to exposure, danger, accident, as well as to temptation. Reason, true morality, religion, sympathy, love, and esthetic enjoyment are but very slightly developed. Everything, in short, suggests the culmination of one stage of life as if it thus represented what was once, and for a very protracted and relatively stationary period, the age of maturity in some remote, perhaps pigmoid, stage of human evolution, when in a warm climate the young of our species once shifted for themselves independently of further parental aid. The qualities now developed are phyletically vastly older than all the neo-atavistic traits of body and soul, later to be superposed like a new and higher story built on to our primal nature. Heredity is so

far both more stable and more secure. The elements of
personality are few, but are well organized and on a
simple, effective plan. The momentum of the paleopsychic traits is great, and they are often clearly dis-
tinguishable from those to be later added. Thus the boy
is father of the man in a new sense in that his qualities
are indefinitely older and existed well compacted un-
told ages before the more distinctly human attributes
were developed. Indeed, there are a few faint indications
set forth in the text of a yet earlier age nodality or
meristic segmentation, as if amid the increased instabili-
ties of health at the age of about six we could still
detect the ripple-marks of an ancient public beach now
lifted high above the tides of a receding shore-line as
human infancy has been prolonged. I have also given
reasons that lead me to the conclusion that, despite its
dominance, the function of sexual maturity and pro-
creative power is peculiarly mobile up and down the age-
line independently of many of the qualities usually so
closely associated with it, so that much that sex created
in the phylum now precedes it in the individual.

Rousseau would leave prepubescent years to nature
and to these primal hereditary impulsions and allow the
fundamental traits of savagery their fling till twelve.
Biological psychology finds many and cogent reasons to
confirm this view if only a proper environment could be
provided. The child revels in savagery, and if its tribal,
predatory, hunting, fishing, fighting, roving, idle, playing
proclivities could be indulged in the country and under
conditions that now, alas! seem hopelessly ideal, they
could conceivably be so organized and directed as to be
far more truly humanistic and liberal than all that the
best modern school can provide. Rudimentary organs of
the soul now suppressed, perverted, or delayed, to crop

out in menacing forms later, would be developed in their season so that we should be immune to them in maturer years, on the principle of the Aristotelian catharsis for which I have tried to suggest a far broader application than the Stagirite could see in his day.

These nativistic and more or less feral instincts can and should be fed and formed. The deep and strong cravings in the individual to revive the ancestral experiences and occupations of the race can and must be met, at least in a secondary and vicarious way, by tales of the heroic virtues the child can appreciate, and these proxy experiences should make up by variety and extent what they lack in intensity. The teacher art should so vivify all that the resources of literature, tradition, history, can supply which represents the crude, rank virtues of the world's childhood that, with his almost visual imagination, reenforced by psychonomic recapitulatory impulses, the child can enter upon his full heritage, live out each stage of his life to the fullest, and realize in himself all its manifold tendencies. Echoes only of the vaster, richer life of the remote past of the race they must remain, but just these are the murmurings of the only muse that can save from the omnipresent dangers of precocity. Thus we not only rescue from the danger of loss, but utilize for further psychic growth the results of the higher heredity, which are the most precious and potential things on earth. So, too, in our urbanized hothouse life, that tends to ripen everything before its time, we must teach nature, although the very phrase is ominous. But we must not, in so doing, wean still more from, but perpetually incite to visit field, forest, hill, shore, the water, flowers, animals, the true homes of childhood in this wild, undomesticated stage from which modern conditions have kidnapped and transported him. Books and reading are distasteful, for the very soul and body cry out for a more active, objective life, and to know nature and man at first hand. These two staples, stories and nature, by these informal methods of the home and the environment constitute fundamental education.

But now another remove from nature seems to be made necessary by the manifold knowledges and skills of our highly complex civilization. We should transplant the human sapling, I concede reluctantly, as early as eight, but not before, to the schoolhouse with its imperfect lighting, ventilation, temperature. We must shut out nature and open books. The child must sit on unhygienic benches and work the tiny muscles that wag the tongue and pen, and let all the others, which constitute nearly half its weight, decay. Even if it be prematurely, he must be subjected to special disciplines and be apprenticed to the higher qualities of adulthood, for he is not only a product of nature, but a candidate for a highly developed humanity. To many, if not most, of the influences here there can be at first but little inner response. Insight, understanding, interest, sentiment, are for the most part only nascent, and most that pertains to the true kingdom of mature manhood is embryonic. The wisest requirements seem to the child more or less alien, arbitrary, heteronomous, artificial, falsetto. There is much passivity, often active resistance and evasion, and perhaps spasms of obstinacy, to it all. But the senses are keen and alert, reactions immediate and vigorous, and the memory is quick, sure, and lasting, and ideas of space, time, and physical causation, and of many a moral and social [concept?] licit and non-licit, are rapidly unfolding. Never again will there be such susceptibility to drill and discipline, such plasticity to habituation, or such ready adjustment to new conditions. It is the age of external and mechanical training. Reading, writing, drawing, manual training, musical technic, foreign tongues and their pronunciation, the manipulation of numbers and of geometrical elements, and many kinds of skill have now their golden hour, and if it passes unimproved, all these can never be acquired later without a heavy handicap of disadvantage and loss. These necessities may be hard for the health of body, sense, mind, as well as for morals, and pedagogic art consists in breaking the child into them betimes as intensively and as quickly as possible with minimal strain and with the least amount of explanation or coquetting for natural interest and in calling medicine confectionery. This is not teaching in its true sense so much as it is drill, inculcation, and regimentation. The method should be mechanical, repetitive, authoritative, dogmatic. The automatic powers are now at their very apex, and they can do and bear more than our degenerate pedagogy knows or dreams of. Here we have something to learn from the schoolmasters of the past back to the middle ages, and even from the ancients. The greatest stress, with short periods and few hours, incessant insistence, incitement, and little reliance upon interest, reason, or work done without the presence of the teacher, should be the guiding principles for pressure in these essentially formal and, to the child, contentless elements of knowledge. These should be sharply distinguished from the indigenous, evoking, and more truly educational factors described in the last paragraph, which are meaty, content-full, and relatively formless as to time of day, method, spirit, and perhaps environment and personnel of teacher, and possibly somewhat in season of the year, almost as sharply as work differs from play, or perhaps as the virility of man that loves to command a phalanx, be a martinet and drill-master, differs from femininity which excels in persuasion, sympathetic insight, story-telling, and in the tact that discerns and utilizes spontaneous interests in the young.

Adolescence is a new birth, for the higher and more completely human traits are now born. The qualities of body and soul that now emerge are far newer. The child comes from and harks back to a remoter past; the adolescent is neo-atavistic, and in him the later acquisitions of the race slowly become prepotent. Development is less gradual and more saltatory, suggestive of some ancient period of storm and stress when old moorings were broken and a higher level attained. The annual rate of growth in height, weight, and strength is increased and often doubled, and even more. Important functions previously non-existent arise. Growth of parts and organs loses its former proportions, some permanently and some for a season. Some of these are still growing in old age and others are soon arrested and atrophy. The old moduli of dimensions become obsolete and old harmonies are broken. The range of individual differences and average errors in all physical measurements and all psychic tests increases. Some linger long in the childish stage and advance late or slowly, while others push on with a sudden outburst of impulsion to early maturity. Bones and muscles lead all other tissues, as if they vied with each other, and there is frequent flabbiness or tension as one or the other leads. Nature arms youth for conflict with all the resources at her command—speed, power of shoulder, biceps, back, leg, jaw,—strengthens and enlarges skull, thorax, hips, makes man aggressive and prepares woman's frame for maternity. The power of the diseases peculiar to childhood abates, and liability to the far more [simple?]* diseases of maturity begins, so that with liability to both it is not strange that the dawn of the ephebic day is marked at the same time by increased morbidity but diminished rates of mortality. Some disorders of arrest and defect as well as of excessive unfoldment in some function, part, or organ may now, after long study and controversy, be said to be established as peculiar to this period, and diseases that are distinctly school- and city-bred abound, with apparently increasing frequency. The momentum of heredity often seems insufficient to enable the child to achieve this great revolution and come to complete maturity, so that every step of the upward way is strewn with wreckage of body, mind, and morals. There is not only arrest, but perversion, at every stage, and hoodlumism, juvenile crime, and secret vice seem not only increasing, but develop in earlier years in every civilized land. Modern life is hard, and in many respects increasingly so, on youth. Home, school, church, fail to recognize its nature and needs and, perhaps most of all, its perils. The cohesions between the elements of personality are loosened by the disparities of both somatic and psychic development, and if there is arrest at any stage or in any part before the higher unity is achieved there is almost sure to be degeneration and reunion on a lower level than before. One of the gravest dangers is the persistent ignoring by femininists of the prime importance of establishing normal periodicity in girls, to the needs of which everything else should for a few years be secondary.

The functions of every sense undergo reconstruction,

---

* Elsewhere Hall remarked that "the characteristic adult diseases to which youth is now becoming liable, without having ceased to be exposed to those of childhood, are often more simple with less evolved symptoms" (*Adolescence*, I, 239).—C. E. S. and C. B.

and their relations to other psychic functions change, and new sensations, some of them very intense, arise, and new associations in the sense sphere are formed. Haptic impressions, appetite for food and drink, and smell are most modified. The voice changes, vascular instability, blushing, and flushing are increased. Sex asserts its mastery in field after field, and works its havoc in the form of secret vice, debauch, disease, and enfeebled heredity, cadences the soul to both its normal and abnormal rhythms, and sends many thousand youth a year to quacks, because neither parents, teachers, preachers, or physicians know how to deal with its problems. Thus the foundations of domestic, social, and religious life are oftenest undermined. Between religion and love God and nature have wrought an indissoluble bond so that neither can attain normality without that of the other. Secondary sexual qualities are shown to have an ever-widening range, and parenthood to mean more with every upward step of development. The youth craves more knowledge of body and mind, that can help against besetting temptations, aid in the choice of a profession, and if his intellect is normal he does not vex his soul overmuch about the logical character of the universe or the ultimate sanction of either truth or virtue. He is more objective than subjective, and only if his lust to know nature and life is starved does his mind trouble him by in-growing. There are new repulsions felt toward home and school, and truancy and runaways abound. The social instincts undergo sudden unfoldment and the new life of love awakens. It is the age of sentiment and of religion, of rapid fluctuation of mood, and the world seems strange and new. Interest in adult life and in vocations develops. Youth awakes to a new world and understands neither it nor himself. The whole future of life depends on how the new powers now given suddenly and in profusion are husbanded and directed. Character and personality are taking form, but everything is plastic. Self-feeling and ambition are increased, and every trait and faculty is liable to exaggeration and excess. It is all a marvelous new birth, and those who believe that nothing is so worthy of love, reverence, and service as the body and soul of youth, and who hold that the best test of every human institution is how much it contributes to bring youth to the ever fullest possible development, may well review themselves and the civilization in which we live to see how far it satisfies this supreme test.

Never has youth been exposed to such dangers of both perversion and arrest as in our own land and day. Increasing urban life with its temptations, prematurities, sedentary occupations, and passive stimuli just when an active, objective life is most needed, early emancipation and a lessening sense for both duty and discipline, the haste to know and do all befitting man's estate before its time, the mad rush for sudden wealth and the reckless fashions set by its gilded youth—all these lack some of the regulatives they still have in older lands with more conservative traditions. In a very pregnant psychological sense ours is an unhistoric land. Our very Constitution had a Minerva birth, and was not the slow growth of precedent. Our ideas of freedom were at the outset fevered by the convulsion of the French Revolution. Our literature, customs, fashions, institutions, and legislation were inherited or copied, and our religion was not a gradual indigenous growth, but both its spirit and forms were imported ready-made from Holland, Rome, England, and Palestine. To this extent we are a fiat nation, and in a very significant sense we have had neither

childhood nor youth, but have lost touch with these
stages of life because we lack a normal development
history. It is not merely that we have no antiquity rich in
material and spiritual monuments that is the best nursery
of patriotism in the young, but our gallery of heroes is
largely composed, not of glorious youth but of sages advanced in age or old in wisdom for their years. Our im-
migrants have often passed the best years of youth or
leave it behind when they reach our shores, and their
memories of it are in other lands. No country is so
precociously old for its years. Few as these are, the senescence of the original American stock is already seen in
abandoned farms and the infecundity of graduates, so
that if our population had been unreplenished from
abroad for the last century we should be to-day not
merely stationary, like France, but retrogressive. In this
environment our young people leap rather than grow
into maturity. Our storm and stress strenuousness too
often imparts at least the narrow nervous intensity of an
individuation that is biologically antagonistic to genesis
and that is less ephebic, as we fondly think it to be, than
ephebeitic. We are conquering nature, achieving a magnificent material civilization, leading the world in the
applications though not in the creation of science, coming to lead in energy and intense industrial and other
activities; our vast and complex business organization
that has long since outgrown the comprehension of professional economists, absorbs ever more and earlier the
best talent and muscle of youth and now dominates
health, time, society, politics, and law-giving, and sets
new and ever more pervading fashions in manners,
morals, education, and religion; but we are progressively
forgetting that for the complete apprenticeship to life,
youth needs repose, leisure, art, legends, romance, ideal-

ization, and in a word humanism, if it is to enter the kingdom of man well equipped for man's highest work in the world. In education our very kindergartens, which outnumber those of any other land, by dogma and hyper-sophistication tend to exterminate the naive that is the glory of childhood. Everywhere the mechanical and formal triumph over content and substance, the letter over the spirit, the intellect over morals, lesson setting and hearing over real teaching, the technical over the essential, information over education, marks over edi-fication, and method over matter. We coquet with chil-dren's likes and dislikes and can not teach duty or the spirit of obedience. In no civilized land is teaching so unprofessional or school boards at such a low level of incompetence. Nowhere are the great traditions of the race so neglected, the high school so oblivious of either the nature or the needs, or both, of the adolescent stage of life. The American college is half universitized with methods and matter prematurely specialized, and half bound to the recitation, marking methods and discipline of the school, while the apex of our educational system is still in Europe, where hundreds of our best graduates go yearly to find the advanced and special training we are still, in most departments, unable to supply.

In religion, which was grafted from an alien ethnic stock, we lack scientific sincerity. Statistics show more sects and more clergymen per capita of population than in any other land, and a rapidly progressive ignorance by the rising generation of the very Bible we profess to revere. Churches, charities, missions abound, but our slums are putrefying sores whose denizens anthropolo-gists believe lower in the moral and intellectual scale than any known race of savages, and the percentages of juvenile crimes and the average age of first commitment

grows steadily earlier. We have vastly simplified politics
by separating Church and State and by our voluntary
system, but we have also permitted a chasm to yawn between our secular and religious life, between science and
theology, till even seminaries for the training of clergymen neglect and even suspect the study of nature as if
God were a hypocrite and did one thing in his works and
said another in his Word, when in fact each supplements
and is an imperfect thing without the other. We try to
impose not only our civilization, but our religion, upon
lower races, even though they are thereby exterminated,
and fail to study the nature and needs of even those we
try to help.

All this is hard on youth, which was better understood
in ancient Greece and Rome than now, for it is profoundly responsive to all these influences. Despite all
this I am an optimist root and core, not merely because
an evolutionist must hold that the best and not the worst
will survive and prevail, but because in most, though not
yet in all, of these fields I see clearly the beginnings of
better things. Even in education and religion, the strong-
holds of conservatism, there are new and better ideals
and efforts, and these are less exceptional and are growing in power and influence and are represented by more
and better men. In vigor, enthusiasm, and courage we are
still young, and our faults are those of youth. Because
they have been great our suffering has been also great,
and pain is the world's best teacher whose lessons are
surest to be laid to heart. The very fact that we think we
are young will make the faith in our future curative,
and we shall one day not only attract the youth of the
world by our unequaled liberty and opportunity, but
develop a mental, moral, and emotional nurture that will
be the best preparation for making the most and the best

of them and for helping humanity on to a higher stage.

As for years, an almost passionate lover of childhood and a teacher of youth, the adolescent stage of life has long seemed to me one of the most fascinating of all themes, more worthy, perhaps, than anything else in the world of reverence, most inviting study, and in most crying need of a service we do not yet understand how to render aright. Socrates knew that there was no such companionship or inspiration. In ministering to it the higher instincts of parenthood culminate and age renews its youth. This should make teaching the most humanistic, the noblest, and the most satisfying vocation of man, as well as the surest safeguard against pessimism. These years are the best decade of life. No age is so responsive to all the best and wisest adult endeavor. In no psychic soil, too, does seed, bad as well as good, strike such deep root, grow so rankly, or bear fruit so quickly or so surely. To love and feel for and with the young can alone make the teacher love his calling and respect it as supreme. That it may directly and indirectly help the young to exploit aright all the possibilities of the years from fourteen to twenty-four and to safe-guard them against the above insidious dangers is the writer's chief desire.

.   .   .

8. The Ideal School
as Based on Child Study*

The following address, delivered before the National Educational Association in 1901, may be regarded as Hall's single most important pronouncement on education. By the turn of the century, his criticism of traditional schooling had matured into a rather detailed program of reforms for educational practice from the kindergarten through the high school. The speech expresses clearly the view that education should be leisurely and respectful of each stage of human development, but it also indicates that Hall's version of the child-centered school placed more emphasis on health, growth, and heredity than on free expression of individual personality.

I shall try in this paper to break away from all current practices, traditions, methods, and philosophies, for a brief moment, and ask what education would be if based solely upon a fresh and comprehensive view of the nature and needs of childhood. Hitherto the data for such a construction of the ideal school have been insufficient, and soon they will be too manifold for any one mind to make the attempt; so the moment is opportune. What follows is based almost solely, point by

* National Educational Association, *Addresses and Proceedings, 1901*, pp. 475–488.

point, upon the study of the stages of child development, and might, perhaps, without presumption be called a first attempt to formulate a practical program of this great movement. In my limited space I can do little more than barely state the conclusions that affect the practical work of teachers.

The school I shall describe exists nowhere, but its methods, unless I err, are valid everywhere. Altho many of its features exist already, and could be pieced together in a mosaic from many lands and ages, it is essentially the school invisible, not made with hands. But, as there is nothing so practical as the truly ideal, altho my school today exists nowhere, it might be organized anywhere tomorrow; and I hope that the most and the least conservative will agree that it is the true goal of all endeavor, and will not differ except as to whether it may be realized at once or only at the end of a long period of labor. I confess that something like this has from the first animated all my own feeble educational endeavors, and that without it I should be without hope and without goal in the world of pedagogy.

Beginning with the deep philosophy often imbedded in words, "school," or "schole," means leisure, exemption from work, the perpetuation of the primaeval paradise created before the struggle for existence began. It stands for the prolongation of human infancy, and the no whit less important prolongation of adolescence. It is sacred to health, growth, and heredity, a pound of which is worth a ton of instruction. The guardians of the young should strive first of all to keep out of nature's way, and to prevent harm, and should merit the proud title of defenders of the happiness and rights of children. They should feel profoundly that childhood, as it comes fresh from the hand of God, is not corrupt, but illustrates the survival of the most consummate thing in the world; they should be convinced that there is nothing else so worthy of love, reverence, and service as the body and soul of the growing child.

Practically, this means that every invasion of this leisure, the provision of a right measure of which is our first duty to youth, has a certain presumption against it, and must justify itself by conclusive reasons. Before we let the pedagog loose upon childhood, not only must each topic in his curriculum give an account of itself, but his inroads must be justified in the case of each child. We must overcome the fetichism of the alphabet, of the multiplication table, of grammars, of scales, and of bibliolatry, and must reflect that but a few generations ago the ancestors of all of us were illiterate; that the invention of Cadmus seemed the sowing of veritable dragon's teeth in the brain; that Charlemagne and many other great men of the world could not read or write; that scholars have argued that Cornelia, Ophelia, Beatrice, and even the blessed mother of our Lord knew nothing of letters. The knights, the élite leaders of the Middle Ages, deemed writing a mere clerk's trick beneath the attention of all those who scorned to muddle their wits with others' ideas, feeling that their own were good enough for them.

Nay more: there are many who ought not to be educated, and who would be better in mind, body, and morals if they knew no school. What shall it profit a child to gain the world of knowledge and lose his own health? Cramming and over-schooling have impaired many a feeble mind, for which, as the proverb says, nothing is so dangerous as ideas too large for it. We are coming to understtand the vanity of mere scholarship and erudition, and to know that even ignorance may be a wholesome poultice for weakly souls; while scribes, sophists, scholastics, and pedants suggest how much of the learning of the past is now seen to be vanity, and how incompetent pedagogs have been as guardians of the sacred things of culture. Thus, while I would abate no whit from the praise of learning and education for all who are fit for them, I would bring discrimination down to the very basis of our educational pyramid.

I. The kindergarten age is from two or three to six or seven. Here, before the ideal school can be inaugurated, we need some work of rescue from the symbolists. Now the body needs most attention, and the soul least. The child needs more mother, and less teacher; more of the educated nurse, and less of the metaphysician. We must largely eliminate, and partly reconstruct, the mother-plays, while transforming and vastly enlarging the repertory of the gifts and occupations. We must develop the ideal nursery, playgrounds, and rooms, where light, air, and water are at their best. The influences of the new hygiene have been felt least here, where they are needed most. The neglect of these basal principles suggests that we have still among us those whose practice implies a belief that any old place is good enough to hatch out beautiful souls, provided only Froebelian orthodoxy of doctrine and method is steadfastly maintained. . . .

The kindergarten should fill more of the day, and should strive to kill time. In the Berlin Institute children sleep at noon in a darkened room, with music, crackers, or even bottles, and thus resist man's enemy, fatigue, and restore paradise for themselves. Part of the cult here should be idleness and the intermediate state of reverie. We should have a good excuse to break into these, and at this age children should be carefully shielded from all suspicion of any symbolic sense. Thus in play, and in play only, life is made to seem real. Imitation should have a far larger scope. Children should hear far more English and better, and in the later years the ear should be trained for French or German. Color should never be taught as such. The children of the rich, generally prematurely individualized or over-individualized, especially when they are only children, must be disciplined and subordinated; while the children of the poor, usually under-individualized, should be indulged. We should lose no syllable of the precious positive philosophy of Froebel, the deepest of all modern educational thinkers; but we must profoundly reconstruct every practical expression that he attempted of his ideas, and must strive to induce at least a few college-trained men and women to turn their attention to the kindergarten, thus making the training schools feel, what they have hitherto known so little of, the real spirit and influence of modern science. Teachers should study every child, not necessarily by any of the current technical methods. They should learn far more than they can teach, and in place of the shallow manikin child of books they should see, know, and love only the real thing. After this metempsychosis, the kindergarten should be, and should become, an integral part of every school system.

II. The age of about seven or eight is a transition period of the greatest interest for science. Then most children have less chewing surface by three or four teeth; there is a year or more of increased danger to the heart; the breath is shorter and fatigue easier; lassitude, nervousness, visual disorders, and cough are somewhat more imminent; and the blood is more often impoverished. The brain has practically finished for life its growth in weight and size; and all work and strain must be reduced. Some important corner in its time of development, not yet fully understood, is turned.

III. At eight or nine there begins a new period, which, for nearly four years, to the dawn of puberty, constitutes a unique stage of life, marked off by many important differences from the period which precedes and that which follows it. During these years there is a decreased rate of growth, so that the body relatively rests; but there is a striking increase of vitality, activity, and power to resist disease. Fatigue, too, is now best resisted, and it is amazing to see how much can be endured. The average child now plays more games, and has more daily activity, in proportion to size and weight, than at any other stage. It would seem, as I have proposed elsewhere with ground for the theory, as tho these four years represented, on the recapitulation theory, a long period in some remote age, well above the simian, but mainly before the historic, period, when our early forebears were well adjusted to their environment. Before a higher and much more modern story was added to human nature, the young in warm climates, where most human traits were evolved, became independent of their parents, and broke away to subsist for themselves at an early age. In this age, which will call the juvenile, the individual boy today is a precious key for the reconstruction of a stage in the history of the race otherwise very obscure.

However this may be, child nature suggests very plainly that this period should be mainly devoted to drill, habituation, and mechanism. The age of reason is only dawning, and is not yet much in order; but discipline should be the watchword here. Writing, and even reading, for instance, should be neglected in our system before eight, and previous school work should focus on stories, the study of nature, and education by play and other activities. Now writing and reading should be first taught with stress. Their nascent period is now beginning. If we teach them before, we are apt to make the average

child a bad writer for life by precocious overemphasis
on the finer muscles. Modern studies show that the zigzag of the eye back and forth along the printed line is as
dangerous as is the too early wigwag of the pen. At best
the strain laid upon these tiny muscles is dangerous. Too
early drill in read-writing is also enormously wasteful,
because intensive effort gives facility now in an amazingly short time. Now first the smaller muscles in the
average child, so important for mind- and will-training,
can bear hard work and much strain. Accuracy, which,
when out of its season, is fraught with so many dangers
for mind and body, is now in order.

Verbal memory is now at its very best, and should be
trained far more than it is. We are now educating the
automatic bases of both mind and morals, and habits are
never so easily formed or made stable. Manual training
and games should be extremely diverse, manifold, and
thoro. It is the time to break in the human colt, which is
by nature, in some sense, the wildest of all wild animals.
If the piano or any other musical instrument is to be
learned, this is the time for drill, especially on scales and
exercises. An instrumentalist's technique is rarely good
if its foundations are not laid in this age. Names, even
technical ones, come now. Drawing, too, should now
come into prominence, beginning in its large and perfectly free form before writing, and only near the end
of the period becoming severely methodic and accurate.
Art training should not result in intimidation, but first
everything should be drawn—battles, fires, shipwrecks,
and railroad accidents, with plenty of human figures and
action, and no angles, straight lines, or regular curves,
which have come very late in the history of the race.
This would make drawing, as it should be, a real expression of the child's soul, and the child should copy what
he, and not what the adult, sees.

The mother-tongue will be the vehicle of nearly all the work of this period; but it will be on the short circuit from ear to mouth, which existed for unknown eons before reading and writing, and not chiefly on the long circuit and, biologically, very recent brain-path from eye to hand. Teachers praise written work in home and at school—compositions, essays, class work; but all these appeal to new and undeveloped powers of nerve and muscle. It is because we try to establish good English upon these foundations, so precarious at this stage, that we have so much and so just complaint of bad English. We ruin both handwriting and idiomatic speech by precocity. The child should live in a world of sonorous speech. He should hear and talk for hours each day; and then he would lay foundations for terse and correct English, and would keep read-writing, as it should forever be, subordinate to hearing and speaking. He would write as he speaks, and we should escape the abomination of bookish talk. At this stage written work should be required far less than at present.

Further, to secure these ends, we must first lay stress upon correct spelling—which is, after all, of far less importance than we think—and also upon correct, adult Addisonian syntax. Good grammar is too much to expect yet. We must strive first for utterance and expression, which may be homely, if only vigorous and adequate. Hence, much that we call slang has its place, and is really a revival of English in its most formative stage. The prim proprieties we idolize are not yet, but it is the hour of delight in cogency of expression. We do not yet know what slang to teach, or how to teach it, but we ought to give the best of it an important place. The boy is not totally depraved because he loves the speech of Chimmie Fadden, of Mr. Ade, or of "The Charwoman," because such language is fresh from the mint where all words were made. Our end is the cultivation of expression, which must bring out clearly and strongly what is in the boy's soul. This expression must be of a kind at least no less effective for other boys than for us. A training that gives the power of writing, or even talking, upon any subject or upon none in particular, is bad and vicious. Children have no right to write unless it is upon some subject that they know, and upon which they feel strongly. Theme and composition should be strictly confined to the fields of interest, and then expression will find or make a vent for itself. Moreover, we should not teach language, as such, or apart from objects, acts, and concrete reality-truth. We must burn most of our language books.

At this stage, arithmetic, so greatly overdone in American schools, should be mechanized, with plenty of mental exercises, and later with rules and processes for written work, with only little attempt at explanation. The elements of geometry, especially on the constructive side, and the metric system should come early, and the rudiments of algebra later. This is the stage, too, for beginning one or two foreign languages. These should always first be taught by ear and mouth. The child has a natural desire to express himself in many other vocal forms than the vernacular, for it is the age when all kinds of gibberish, dog Latin, and inventive words culminate. It represents the stage when human speech evolved fastest. If these languages are taught earlier, they jeopardize idiomatic English; if later, they are never pronounced or used with precision, and are not immediate vehicles of thought. Psychology has shown that speech is greatly reinforced by appeals to the eye, not in the form of the written or printed word, but thru pictures, and that even color intensifies the linguistic effect. Many a French or

German word that could not otherwise be recalled is reproduced, or first taught more permanently, if the object or picture is shown, or the appropriate action is performed at the same instant. Books should be by no means discarded, but the chief stress should be laid on the oral work and thought. The object should be brought into immediate action without the intervention of the English word.

As to the dead languages, if they are to be taught, Latin should be begun not later than ten or eleven, and Greek never later than twelve or thirteen. Here both object and method are very different. These languages are taught thru English, and the eye-hand circuit should have much more prominence. Word-matching and translation are the goal. The chief reason why the German boy of fifteen or sixteen in *Unter Secunda* does so easily here what seems to us prodigious is because he is taught to study; and the teacher's chief business in class is not to hear recitations, but to study with the boys. One of the best of these teachers told me that the boy should never see a dictionary or even a vocabulary, but the teacher must be a "pony." The pupil should never be brought face to face with an unknown sentence, but everything must be carefully translated for him; he must note all the unknown words from the teacher's lips and all the special grammatical points, so that home study and the first part of the next lesson will be merely repetitions of what the teacher had told and done.

The modern school geography should be reduced to about one-fourth or even one-eighth of its present volume. It is too often a mosaic of geology, topography, physical geography, botany, zoölogy, anthropology, meteorology, and astronomy. The facts of each of these sciences, however, are not taught in their natural or logical order; but the associations are mainly those of place and contiguity, not of similarity and cause. Even in these days of correlation of studies the facts of these sciences are separated from their logical connection with each other; and by the use of a more fortuitous local association the reason is injured. Our geographies do not respect the unity of the child's mind. Their facts are connected neither with each other nor with the nascent stages of growth. The interest in primitive man and animals culminates from nine to ten; that in trade and governmental parts of geography comes from sixteen to twenty. The geographies of the last two or three years have mitigated, but by no means healed, these evils; and, as we speak of Turkey as "the sick man of Europe," we may still speak of geography as the sick subject of our curriculum.

Instead of reverencing this relic of mediaevalism, as its history shows it to be, we should greatly reduce the time given to it, and should first teach *Heimatskunde;* make maps more abundant, but more incidental to every topic, especially history; develop and teach elementary and illustrated anthropology and zoölogy, broadening to elementary astronomy, geology, meteorology, and botany, taught by and for themselves to bring out their disciplinary value, and so on in ways I have here no space to dwell upon. When we have reduced the enormous time now given to geography, the elements of each of these sciences will be taught in primers—some of which are now begun before the end of this period—which will continue the nature work of the period before seven or eight.

The hand is in a sense never so near the brain as now; knowledge never so strongly tends to become practical; muscular development never so conditions mental. Muscle-training of every kind, from play up to manual work, must now begin. Instead of the Swedish or other curriculized and exactly finished objects made, we should have a curriculum of toys at first and of rude scientific apparatus later, where everything will focus more upon the ulterior use of the object than upon the process of making it. All these things will be chosen from the field of the child's interests.

Singing will be prominent in the ideal school at this age; but far more time will be given to rote singing than to singing from notes, especially at first. The chief aim will be, not to develop the power to read music, important as the place of this is, but to educate the sentiments, and especially to attune them to love of home, nature, fatherland, and religion—the four chief themes of song in all ages, past and present. Music is the language of the feelings, just as speech is of the intellect. It is as absurd to teach notes to children before they can sing well as it would be to teach them reading before they can speak. The object of musical education in the public school is to express and train the emotions, and, thru these, the will and character; to preform joys and conduct, and not to make musicians.

Reason is still very undeveloped. The child's mind is at a stage when there is little in it that has not been brought in by way of sense. We must open wide the eye-gate and the ear-gate. "Show," "demonstrate," and "envisage" should be our watchwords, not "explain." We can easily make casuists and prigs, but we jeopardize thereby the ultimate vigor of reason. Hence we should explain very little. Even with respect to morals and conduct the chief duty of the child at this age is to obey. In most cases to try to explain brings self-consciousness and conceit. This method is the resource of teachers and

parents whose personality is deficient in authoritative-
ness. Obedience should still be a law, if not a passion. If
it is lacking, this is due to imperfect character or perverted methods in adults.

In fine, this is the age for training, with plenty of
space and time, however, for spontaneity and voluntary
action. The good teacher is a true *Pedotrieb,* or boy
driver. He needs some method, but much more matter.
He or she finds relatively little sentiment, but much
selfishness, bound up in the hearts of children at this age.
One of the chronic errors of too fond mothers and of
modern teachers is to overestimate the capacities of
children, especially boys, at this age for sympathy with
adult feelings or interests. The world we live in is not
theirs. We are "Olympians," and can enforce our will
because we are stronger. We must be tolerated and re-
spected, and must be treated with all the forms of respect and obedience that we require; but the interest of
children at this age is almost exclusively in each other,
and in each other's ways, not in adults. This breaks out
suddenly, but just later.

Just before this period ends, boys and girls in the ideal
school will be chiefly, tho not exclusively, placed under
the care of teachers of their own sex. At the close of this
period the ideal child, ideally trained, will be first of all
helpful and active in body and mind; will read and
write well; will know a great deal about the different
aspects of nature in his home environment; will not be
bookish, but will already know a few dozen well-chosen
books; will understand and read simple French and German; and will perhaps have a good start in Latin and
Greek. Some buds of specialization will have begun to
bourgeon. This child will be able to play several dozen
games; will know something of a number of industries;

and will be able to make several dozen things that he is interested in. He will be respectful, tho not particularly affectionate, and will take pleasure in obeying those he likes, and perhaps more in disobeying those he dislikes. He will have attempted a number of organizations for teams, and will have formed a few societies, but all will have been transient. He will have some acquaintance with most of the story roots and literary monuments of the world, perhaps two or three score in number. He will sing, and will draw almost anything, not well, but intelligibly and without affectation.

Lastly, the ideal teacher at this age will be the captain of the child's soul; will be able to do some things with his or her body that the child cannot; will be able to answer most of the questions suggested by the field, the forest, the beach, the street, and their denizens; will suggest plays and umpire games; will perhaps know a little of coaching, but will be a stern disciplinarian, genial withal, but rigorous and relentless in his exactions, and intolerant of all scamped work; will love occasional excursions and expeditions; will perhaps sing, play, and draw a little; will be able to do something expertly well; and, as perhaps the culminating quality, will have a repertory of the greatest stories the human race has ever told or heard.

The ideal story-teller will prefer twilight or evening, with at least the dim light that gives the imagination a chance over sense, perhaps with flickering flames to objectify his scenes. He will then weave the almost hypnotic charm of "Once upon a time." Thus he will repeat the tales of Ulysses, Orestes, Siegfried, Thor, King Arthur and his knights, the wanderings of Aeneas and Telemachus, perhaps some tales from one or other of the great ethnic Bibles, perhaps Dante, some of the soul-transforming myths of Plato—such as Atlantis, the cave, the two steeds—Hercules at the cross-roads, perhaps some legends from ancient India, Reynard the Fox, something from Grimm and Simrock. It is a grievous wrong to permit any child to satisfy the legal requirements of school attendance without some knowledge of these things. I believe in the ethical virtue of these things almost as I believe in the Bible, for they sink deep and transform. They are the Bible of childhood, and we must not withhold them. A story brings a vast body of related facts and persons to a sharp focus. This is what most modern methods of correlation fail to attain. Such stories discipline the heart and the attention at the same time, and implant a taste for good reading and a distaste for bad. Finally, the teacher should have good manners, a uniform disposition, much joy of life, and sympathy with just this age. Some persons are made to love children in this stage most of all; some, to love adolescents; the interest of most and their service to the young are almost always specialized; and none can be equally good teachers or parents for all ages.

IV. Adolescence is a term now applied to a pretty well-marked stage, beginning at about thirteen with girls and a year later with boys, and lasting about ten years, to the period of complete sexual maturity. It is subdivided into pubescence, the first two years; youth proper, from sixteen to twenty in boys and perhaps fifteen to nineteen in girls; and a finishing stage thru the early twenties. The first stage is marked by a great increase in the rate of growth in both height and weight. It is a period of greater susceptibility to sickness for both sexes; but this vulnerability is due to the great changes, and the death-rate is lower in the early teens than at any other age. It is the time when there is the most rapid development of the heart and all the feelings and emotions. Fear, anger, love, pity, jealousy, emulation, ambition, and sympathy are either now born or springing into their most intense life. Now young people are interested in adults, and one of their strong passions is to be treated as if they were mature. They desire to know, do, and be all that becomes a man or woman. Childhood is ending, and plans for future vocations now spring into existence, and slowly grow definite and controlling.

There is often a new and exquisite sensitiveness to every breath of criticism, praise, or blame. All are anxious to know whether they are inferior or superior to others. There may be observed both a new diffidence and a new self-assertion. The largest percentage of criminals is found in the later teens, and at this time most conversions occur also. Both pleasure and pain are vastly intensified. Pugnacity becomes very strong, as does the instinct for showing off. The large muscles and then the small develop rapidly, but are at first unenduring and clumsy. The heart and arteries are suddenly enlarged, and the blood pressure is increased. Blushing is greatly developed. Nature puts body and soul on their mettle. Heredity chiefly, and environment next, determine whether the individual can cross this *pons* successfully; whether he can molt into maturity completely without loss or arrest. New friendships and new secrets are formed; the imagination blossoms; the soul is never so sensitive to all the aspects of nature; music, which may have been studied before, is now felt; the excelsior motive or the developmental push upward makes this the very best and richest season of life. New curiosities, amounting to intellectual hungers, are felt.

Thus again a few years or even months give us a new kind of being, which demands a new environment, new methods, and new matter. Instinct, now so much wiser than reason, feels this break of continuity. It is the age when the majority leave school forever and begin life for themselves. The apex of the runaway and truancy curve is here. It is the age of spring fever, when previous life seems dead, and the soul would molt it and be done with it. It is the most vulnerable and difficult of all periods after infancy, the severest test of parent, teacher, and pedagogical methods. It is the point where, in the sequential history of the race, education has begun in every indigenous race, and from which it widens up toward the university and down toward the kindergarten, just in proportion as civilization advances and the mass of culture material grows. What we shall do with the hobbledehoys, *Backfische,* larrikins, is the oldest problem of education, and one answer is plain: We must first study them. This process has been begun, and has yielded a few results, some very clear and some still uncertain.

First of all, the drill and mechanism of the previous period must be gradually relaxed, and an appeal must be made to freedom and interest. Individuality must have a far longer tether. We must, and can, really teach nothing that does not appeal to interests deep enough to make it seem of almost supreme value in the world. We can no longer coerce and break, but must lead and inspire. To drill merely is now to arrest. Each individual must be studied and made a special problem, if his personality is to come to full maturity. Hence, there must be a wide range of elective study for those who continue at school. Boys can hereafter rarely do their best work under female teachers, however well equipped these may be mentally. They feel their manhood, and need the dominance of male influences.

In the ideal school system the sexes will now, for a

time at least, pretty much part company. They are beginning to differ in every cell and tissue, and girls for a time need some exemption from competition. They have more power than boys to draw upon their capital of physical energy and to take out of their system more than it can afford to lose, for the individuals of one generation can consume more than their share of vigor at the expense of posterity. In soul and body girls are more conservative; males vary, differentiate, and are more radical. Reproduction requires a far larger proportion of body and function in females. Now the leaders of the new education for girls recommend training them for self-support, assuming that, if wifehood and motherhood come, those who have received such a training can best take care of themselves. This assumption is radically wrong and vicious, and should be reversed. Every girl should be educated primarily to become a wife and mother, and, if this is done wisely and broadly, the small minority who remain single will, with this training, be best able to care for themselves.

A third conclusive and far-reaching principle is that at no stage of life is the power to appreciate and apprehend so very far ahead of the power to express. Hence we should let up on examinations; we should cast our bread upon the waters, knowing that it will be found after many days, because so sensitized is the soul now that nothing is lost. Mental and moral teaching and influences sink at once too deep to be reproduced in examinations of the present type, without injury to both mind and will. There is nothing in the whole environment to which the adolescent nature does not keenly respond. Neither you nor I, however specialized our knowledge, know anything really worth knowing, the substance of which cannot be taught now if we have pedagogical tact;

but, if we wait for its reproduction in the pupil, we starve and retard his soul. Hence facts, ideas, laws, and principles should be in the very atmosphere, for they are now the ingenuous youth's native breath, his vital air. He is all insight and receptivity; he has just entered the stage of apprenticeship to life; he has awakened to it as at a second birth, and has found all things new and glorious.

Yet another change is well defined. Whereas previously the pupil could work with some skill and accuracy, now body and mind are both again so plastic and unformed that they are clumsy, and precision and finish cannot be bought except at too great a price. The teacher's cue is now to graft the soul all over with buds and scions, and not to try to gather a harvest. The mind has laid aside its power to finish and elaborate. It can rudely assimilate everything by turns, but nothing well. The fundamental system of the body, which consists of the large muscles and not the small, and which therefore makes coarse, massive movements and not exact ones, has now its innings; and the fundamentals of the soul, which are instinct and intuition, and not pure intellect, are now in season. We must lay new and larger foundations.

But, more specifically, what do these changes involve in the ideal school of the future? The transition from the grammar to the high school in this country corresponds far better than the European system to the need of changed environment at the age of fourteen; and this constitutes a rare opportunity, which has, however, been thrown away. Altho education, as we have seen, begins here, and many races have no other than a brief training at the dawn of the ephebic period, by a strange irony of fate secondary education has more or less lapsed to a mere link. Its functions are partly those of preparation for college, and are partly shaped by the mere momentum of the lower grades. The high school has lost its independence, and of all stages and grades has least interest in the large problems of education, namely, what to teach and how, in order to develop the nascent periods during the teens and to save powers now new-born in most profusion, but sure to be atrophied or perverted if not studied with tact and federated with individual adaptation.

For all these problems as a class, high-school teachers care less than those of any other grade, if, indeed, they suspect their existence. For them adolescence is just a stage when children are so much farther along than in the grammar school, and know so much less than they must to enter college. For such teachers the task is simply to convert their pupils into freshmen, and they await with hope or fear the assignment of their stint in the form of college requirements. They have abandoned all initiative; have renounced their birthright of interpreting, and ministering to, the needs of one stage of life; have had little professional training; have little interest in education in the large meaning of that term; and care little for work of the lower grades. Their motto almost seems to be, *Non vitae sed scholae discimus.* The result is that boys, who insist more on their own individuality, leave the high school: in the country at large about 60 per cent. of its pupils are now girls. Noble ideals are gone; the independent function of the secondary stage of education is almost abandoned; and the pupil and teacher devote themselves to a routine of tasks in an artificial program imposed by the will of others, and fitting, not for the world, but for college. The pupils do not regard their work as set on a basis which gives it a value and meaning in itself to which each day contributes. Nothing can be done then until the high school takes a stronger hold on the interests and affections of the pupil.

At the sessions of the representatives of New England high schools and colleges, all the discussions and interests center more and more in the details of how to fit in this and that study, and whether a little more or less should be required or methods tinkered. College requirements, and suggestions how they may be best met, have ceased to be educational themes in any large sense. It is high time to reverse this relation. The college depends on the high school, and not *vice versa*. The latter should declare its independence, and proceed to solve its own problems in its own way; it should strive to fit for life those whose education stops here, and should bring the college to meet its own demands. It should ask again how best to feed the interests and capacities peculiar to this age; how to fill and develop mind, heart, will, and body, rather than how to distill a budget of prepared knowledge decreed by professors who know no more of the needs of this age than teachers of other grades. The current "link" theory and practice interfere, moreover, with the natural selective functions; favor uniformity and inflexibility; and ignore the needs of the majority of high-school pupils who go no farther.

Under this condition it is idle to study adolescence or to plan for it, because nothing worth while can be done; although the inverse relation I plead for would be vastly to the interests of the colleges, and would in a few years greatly increase their classes and the efficacy of the whole system. Few institutions of modern civilization so distrust human nature as does the modern American high school, when under college domination. For lower grades the law of compulsory attendance is analogous

to a high protective tariff, which removes the stimulus to
better methods of manufacture, and interferes with the
law of competition which is the mainspring of evolution. The high school is no less effectively protected
against the currents of new ideas, and is left to be a vic-
tim of tradition, routine, the iron law of mechanism.
It takes the easiest way by working under the shelter and
dictation of the college above and on the momentum of
the grammar school below. This, I believe, accounts for
the rapidly decreasing numbers as we go up the high-
school classes; for the decreasing proportion of high-
school boys who go to college; for the preponderance of
girls in the high school; and for the educational apathy
of the high-school teacher, who is prone to all the narrowness and affectation of the specialist, without his
redeeming virtue of productiveness in research.

The teacher must teach more, and know more; he must
be a living fountain, not a stagnant pool. He should not
be a dealer in desiccated, second-hand knowledge, a mere
giver-out and hearer of lessons. That is the chief and
humiliating difference between our secondary teachers
and those abroad, who are mostly doctors of philosophy,
as they should be. If we could move many university
professors to the college, many college professors to the
high school, many high-school teachers to the grammar
school, and some grammar-school teachers, with at least
a sprinkling of college graduates, into the kindergarten,
it would do much. In the German and French schools the
teacher is one who knows a great deal about his subject
and is nearer to original sources; who tells the great
truths of the sciences almost like stories; and who does
not affect the airs and methods of the university professor. Very many secondary teachers are masters and
authorities. Here, most of our university pedagogy is a

mere device for so influencing high-school principals and teachers as to correlate curricula, in order to corral in students, and little interest is taken in the grammar grades, and none in the kindergarten.

I have spoken frankly, and have dealt only with general principles over a vast field, far too large to be adequately discussed here. I have carefully avoided all details, altho I have fully worked them out on paper at great length, for each topic to the close of the high-school period or the age of nineteen, when physical growth is essentially completed. This material will soon appear in a volume. The chief petition in my daily prayer now is for a millionaire. With the means at hand, I have no shadow of doubt or fear but that in five years from the date of any adequate gift we shall be able to invite all interested to a system of education, covering this ground, which will be a practical realization of much present prophecy, and which will commend itself even to the most conservative defenders of things as they are and have been, because the best things established will be in it. But it will be essentially pedocentric rather than scholiocentric; it may be a little like the Reformation, which insisted that the sabbath, the Bible, and the church were made for man and not he for them; it will fit both the practices and the results of modern science and psychological study; it will make religion and morals more effective; and, perhaps above all, it will give individuality in the school its full rights as befits a republican form of government, and will contribute something to bring the race to the higher maturity of the superman that is to be, effectiveness in developing which is the highest and final test of art, science, religion, home, state, literature, and every human institution.

9. The High School as the People's College*

In 1902, Hall elaborated the theme of the ideal school, providing more detail on the sort of high school suited to adolescence. Noting that the public high school sent relatively few of its students on to higher education, Hall concluded that a thorough reform of its aims, methods, and course of study was needed. The "people's college" should de-emphasize the classical languages and mathematics and seize on the physical vigor and latent idealism of youth by giving more attention to heroic literature, evolutionary science, and vocational training.

Education may fit the youth to live in the past, the present, or the future; and systems may be distinguished according to the relative influence of each. In the Renaissance, which was the golden dawn of secondary education, the past ruled. The literature and life of ancient Greece and Rome were revived. Sturm's goal was so to train his pupils that if they were suddenly transported to Rome or Athens they would be at home in the language, history, and customs. The vernacular was formed on the model of the ponderous Ciceronian sentence which set all the fashions in style. Latin was the

* National Educational Association, *Addresses and Proceedings,* 1902, pp. 260–268.

language of the school and the playground. The games and the whole atmosphere harked back to antiquity. There was no contemporary literature, history, science deemed worth while. The fashion and the earmark of culture was to write a style interlarded with classical quotations and allusions. Liberal education consisted in reviving the dead past, and the results were remarkable. The boys became young Greeks and Romans.

How have we fallen away! Years of the study of Latin and Greek do not accomplish what months did then. Methods and results alike are degenerate. The baby Latin and Greek taught in our high schools is but a sanctified relic, the ghost of a ghost; and we find today almost every degree of degeneration from the golden age of secondary classical training. This is confessed even by its representatives in the German *Gymnasia,* where the old ideal is still best maintained in the modern world. An informed writer says that this high-school fetich no more revives antique culture than the soil is fertilized by the smell of the dung-cart driven over it; says that he has been incapacitated for his duties in modern life by the seductions of this phantom, and that his grandfather, the president of the United States, was injured by it, altho, pathetic to relate, he always praised it. The German emperor, in his famous rescript, declared it a shame to the modern youth to excel in Latin composition, and declared that he would have no more *Gymnasia* or Professor *Hintzpeters.* Norway forbids and Sweden has almost banished it from the secondary schools. The well-known Frankfurt method substitutes three years of modern languages for this, and finds at the end of five years pupils have more than made up. Mr. Reddie at Abbotsholme, Lietz at Ilsenburg, Demolins at L'école de Roche, have set back fires that are spreading in their respective countries. Booker T. Washington says the two chief desires of the colored youth during all the reconstruction period were to hold office and to study Latin, and that his lifework for his race has been directed against these two evils.

I raise no question of the great value of these studies for those who go deeply into them. I acknowledge an inestimable debt to antiquity. I believe in humanistic culture. But when I find that during the past ten years, in which our high-school population has more than doubled, Latin has increased from 34 per cent. in 1890 to about 50 per cent. in 1900, while the proportion of those who go to college has decreased from 14 to 11 per cent., I believe the educational waste and devastation, in view of the growing claims and growing neglect of modern subjects, are calamitous to the point of pathos.

Despite vigorous denials, I am convinced that the general complaint of imperfect command of the mother-tongue by high-school youth is due largely to translation English, and I cite the report of the Harvard entrance committee which challenges comparison for sloven[li]ness and mutilation of good English style; and yet it is just at this stage, before the power to read without translating is acquired, that a recent writer says the chief benefit for the vernacular is acquired. Most high-school Latinists do not go on to college. Beginnings that leave abandoned tracks in the brain because there is no relation to after-life are evil. Moreover, it is a purely formal discipline with almost no content as now taught. Its practical relations to life, arts, literature, which are so magnified, are of the slightest. Thirty-four per cent. of those who drop out of the high school do so from loss of interest and enchantment, and this is true mainly with the classics.

What keeps these studies alive? First, their traditional

respectability. The high school was the Latin school, and children and parents feel they have launched on a higher stage in development when they are known to be students of Latin and perhaps algebra; especially is this true of Catholics. Moreover, Latin is often required in the first high-school year, still more often strongly advised. Again, it is probably the easiest and cheapest of all subjects to teach. I would undertake to hire a hundred female Latin teachers at shorter notice and for less cost than in any other topic. Again, college requirements and possibilities are an enormous bribe, and our secondary education is losing its independence by the excessive interference and dominance from above; and, finally, one can teach Latin and break in the youthful mind with more authority and ease than in any other topic. The voice of its defects is either hoarse or thin and piping with age. They are the rear guard in the retreat of what was once a great army; but the grasp of this dead hand from the tombs of culture must be relaxed.

How different when we turn from the too exclusive dominance of the past, which has its stronghold in that most conservative of all institutions, perhaps the church not excepted, to the training that fits for modern life in the present! Happily there is always a rapidly growing tendency in every modern race and nation to make its schools in its own image, and to measure their efficiency by how well they fit for the domestic, social, political, industrial present. It is the burden of the German Kaiser's complaint that the schools do not give him good soldiers, well-trained civil servants, competent administrators, intelligent patriots. The ministry, and still more the law, show progressive inadequacy to the demands laid upon them. Mr. Kidd would test schools by the maximal social efficiency. Our own Dr. Harris measures them by the thoroness with which they prepare for the life of state, church, school, and home. We often imagine the enormous stimulus which would follow if educational requirements were as thoroly enforced here for our 120,000 office-holders as they are in Germany, where, to fill the lowest office, one must have attained a certain state schooling, and each higher stage up thru secondary and university grades opens the possibility of higher and higher government appointments. Business and trades also have their requirements.

To interpret "fitting for life" to mean fitting for the best service in existing institutions of the present, altho immeasurably better than fitting for the past, brings, along with all its inspiration, a growing danger of narrowness. It is a Roman postulate dear to organizers and to those who love to impart prepared knowledge, which the mature intellect selects as most useful. It tends to utilitarianism and is illiberal, whether one is fitting for a trade or for college. Standards are external, and the question is: Will it pay, whether in money or in passing examinations? Those who thus conceive education place the social organism first and subordinate the individual to his place in it. Citizenship bulks large compared with manhood and womanhood. Their philosophy of education, if they have one, is clear and convenient. Napoleon organized French education on this plan that it might give him good officials. Three-fourths of the students of the *lycées* look forward to snug little berths, and those who fail, after weary years of eating their hearts out, turn to independent careers from necessity, as a last resort. An office, with badge, uniform, and permanence, is the French parent's ideal. The hopelessness of reforms in secondary education here is due to the excessive surveillance of the school to the needs of the social and political community. The French boy's spur to graduate early is that he may get in the line of promotion in office, which is always by seniority. Families have to be small, because every addition diminishes each child's share of the parents' property, and no girl and few boys can marry without a dowry. The French schoolboy thus foresees everything in his career at the start, save only the date of his death, unless he fails of appointment and remains a candidate for starvation. In China the evils of this system are more fully developed. Demolins well says: "That system of education which attempts to adapt the young to existing institutions is bad and must fail." It tends to make young graduates tuft-hunters and place-seekers, hoping to secure by influence soft berths, instead of launching forth and carving out a career for themselves. They are always fitting for something, accumulating learning for the highest market, and the aroma of the trade school penetrates academic halls and causes premature, undue specialization.

But there is a third muse, the inspirations of which are now more and more felt, which teaches that the school should be the bud and nursery of the world that is to be; that it should not be made in the image of the present, but should fit man for the next stage of development in the race and nation. In the present age of rapid transition and expansion of our race, the future and the ideal must be more dominant than ever before, or we are dwarfed as a nation. This is a good age to be young in. It is the psychologic moment for new pedagogic aims, topics, and methods, when the pulses of the old are quickened as with a new adolescence. Our children must not be trained merely to defend the old fortresses of civilization, but to carry on offensive and defensive warfare in fields as yet unexplored. We must not only augment present, but projected, efficiency. Altho the method of fitting for the future is to overflow the needs of the present, just as outgrowing our old soul is the best way to molt a new one in an age of moving equilibrium, we must remember that very much that we praise is deciduous; that the present is not a finality; is a germ and not a blossom, and still less a fruit; and that, unless we are to be jingoes and chauvinists, after knowing the spirit of the age, we must quite as often oppose as serve it. Youth is prophecy, for which its ideals are proverbially the best material. The battles of nations are sometimes won decades before on the school playgrounds. "As Oxford feels and thinks," runs the old slogan, "England thirty years later will act, for it is here that her history is preformed." Otherwise we turn out graduates like the man born just too late, who spent his after-life trying to make up for the last quarter of an hour. Thus we teachers must always, and especially today, be dual personalities: on the one hand, held to our primary organism, and careful that no good in the past be lost; but, on the other, smitten with a divine discontent with the present and its works and ways, trying to make our own lives more honest and exemplary, and more hopeful and worth living, because we give life to others, and worshiping the god of the present but as an ex- or emeritus deity when the god of the future shows his face.

What will the high school, as the people's college, be and do? I answer—if you will pardon summary phrases for the sake of brevity:

First, it will teach English with the chief stress, not upon language or form, but upon content, literature, history, and science. It will not exclude the Bible—man's chief text-book in psychology, human nature, self-knowledge, self-reverence, and self-control; its prophecies as the best school of the future; its appeal to faith as the substance of things hoped for; its poetry of nature, of morals, aesthetics, and of the true piety of the heart as that out of which are the issues of life; as that which follows the order of the soul's unfoldment thru boyhood, adolescence, maturity, and old age, for which one American university already gives credits on admission.

Second, the people's college will teach oratory. I have found fourteen widely used books on rhetoric which dilate on punctuation, paragraphing, the subtleties of style and good use, proofreading, correct and incorrect use of idioms, theories of poetic structure, narration, description, and, above all, composition, which A. S. Hill's *Rhetoric* says is the "main business of the teacher of English." "Rhetoric is proper words in proper places, and the teacher must be all the time on the watch for errors," altho not one student in ten thousand has anything to say; and rhetoric, it is said, does "not teach or imply thinking clearly." Now, the very word "rhetoric" means oratory. To Aristotle it meant giving truth the superiority which belongs to it by its nature. It means the art of influencing conduct with the truth sent home by the living man. Rome knew no other education, and only in her decadence did rhetoric of our type arise, with its trifling, artificial, sophistical way. Some of this the English of the people's college should restore.

Third, the drama at its best is an incomparable school of life. The characters stand out clear and distinct; both they and the action are far easier to comprehend than in life, where all is more complex. Dramatic reading suits youth, and very much can be done in a single high-school year, even without a school theater, if we would only abandon our senseless worship of notes. I visited a high-school class which had spent three weeks on *Othello,* not one of whom yet knew how the story ended. The good drama is moral, because it rewards the good and punishes the villains. The lid of conventionality is taken off human nature, which is seen in its pure types, and a wholesome carthasis [*sic*] against evil is applied. There is always conflict, collision, and passion, which suits youth and makes the theater often truer than history, teaching the power that makes for righteousness. The decay of the modern theater from its happy ideal is hardest on youth.

Another content study in English work should be the great mediaeval epics. Quintilian said that such "contribute more to the unfoldment of students than all the treatises that all the rhetoricians ever wrote." High-school boys have passed the age of chief interest in Homer content, but it is the age of King Arthur, the Sangreal, Parsifal, Sir Galahad, Siegfried, and Lohengrin. This is the quarry where Chaucer, Shakespeare, Scott, Tennyson, Wagner, Ibsen, and scores of artists have found their inspiration. The theme of it all is chivalry and honor—the noblest thing in feudalism. It means reverence for womanhood, pity, valor, loyalty, courtesy, munificence, justice, obedience, and heroism. Here grew the ideals of the gentleman, who was tender, generous, and helpful as well as brave. Morals and aesthetics have never been blended in a way which better fits the nature and needs of youth.

Thus the purpose of literature in the high school is supremely ethical, and the talk of art for art's sake here is degeneration. The receptive faculties are indefinitely ahead of the creative, hence to read, and, above all, see, should take great precedence over composition, which comes hard and late; unless we wish to teach youth fluency with nothing that burns or is worth saying.

Next to English in the people's college should come

science, which teaches love and knowledge of nature—
the great mother of us all, and from which religion, art,
and literature, as well as science, have sprung. The
sciences chosen should be those that give largeness of view
rather than precocious accuracy, and we should remember that man was a naturalist long before the laboratory.
Youthful curiosity always strangely gravitates to frontier
questions, where we are all children, and loves to play
with great ideas—force, atoms, vast astronomic space,
and geological time; is curious about remote lands,
primitive people, strange animals and plants, the origins
of things, and perhaps their end and destiny. The high
school has laid too great and early emphasis upon physics, which, in the last few years, owing to college forcing
and bad methods, as I have elsewhere pointed out, has
declined. First, high-school science should always include
the elements of astronomy. Natural curiosity about the
heavens is now at its strongest and best, and the result is
reverence, for "the undevout astronomer is mad." Very
little celestial mathematics is needed; that came late;
little calculation of eclipses or tides, or minute work with
noon marks, but a meaty body of facts about nebulae,
the number of stars, the distances of those that are most
remote, their motions in systems very different from our
own; collisions, comets, the dead planets; the sun and
moon, than which Plato and Aristotle knew no higher
gods; the hero-ology of astronomy, which has had its
saints and martyrs; its epochs, its culture-history, and
astrology; and what the great astronomers are now
doing.

Again, geology should have a place. It takes little children out of doors, interests them in landscape, teaches
them to understand it; glaciers and the ice-age; the dynamic side of air, water, heat, and life from the palaeo-

zoic age down; a little structural geology, with the composition of rocks, ripple marks, beaches, and shores; the history of the globe from its origin; something of cartography, with knowledge as well as love of the face of nature; large views of time, and how the ascending orders of plants and animals arose. This is far harder to teach than chemistry and physics, and the nose cannot be held to the grindstone so steadily and securely. It requires a larger body of information and more real teaching.

Biology should certainly have a place. Not necessarily the technique of histology or the microscope; less about the cell, and more about natural history than nomenclature or classification. The fertilization of plants by insects and flowers opens a great opportunity for the skillful teacher to instill great moral lessons at an age when they are most needed, and with most unconsciousness. While migration, habitat, economic and human aspects; our knowledge of animal instinct; noxious and healthful plants, insects, and animals; domestication; nests and homes; laws of growth in man, and his general anatomy and physiology, should have place, with themes wisely chosen from anthropology.

These three are real or substantial content studies, while all language work and even mathematics are relatively formal. I would by no means exclude mathematics or modern languages, but would give them a secondary and more elective place in a high school that is to be truly American.

The third group of topics in a secondary system that fits present nature and needs is distinctly motor or efferent, and involves the training of the muscles and the will, more or less inseparable at this age. I have no space here to describe how either the games or the manual training should be conducted in detail, but will only

state its goal and ideal, which is efficiency. Here boys
should be rated by what they can do. There must be the
germs and educative extracts of just as many trades and
industries as possible. On this practical side no better
ideal can be conceived than that of fitting young men for
success in the newer and more unsettled parts of the
country or in our new colonies. Horace Greeley's "Go
west, young man" fits for life in a way almost ideal at
adolescence. The younger sons of British nobility and
the middle classes are beginning thus to be best trained.
If we do not fit our youths for the geographical frontier,
we should inspire them with the idea of beginning at the
bottom, so low they cannot sink lower, but where every
change must be a rise. They should take their places between younger and less trained men, and trust to merit,
with blood and iron enough in them to scorn sedentary
ideals or the easiest way, and be, in Daudet's phrase, a
struggleforlifeur. We must not forget that agriculture,
mining, farming, trade, and commerce are the basis of all
national life, and in a sense everything else is dependent
on and parasitic to these. The mighty engine of business
absorbs more and more of our best talent and requires
ever greater energy, larger knowledge, breadth of view,
and, especially, penetration into the future. It dominates
statesmanship and the professions; its prizes are the
greatest. Thus trained, our youths will plunge into
strenuous life of achievement, and every man-Jack of
them will want to bring his whole self to bear where he
can compete and meet the verdict of his peers. If he is
truly American, he will want to begin at the bottom, because he has a fundamental instinct of thoroness and
fundamentality, and the wise parent will at the critical
moment cut the navel string and toss the young out into
the current of life to sink or swim. The Abbotsholme

boys found their school a rubbish heap, overgrown with weeds, and took pleasure for years in cleaning it up. The man who means railroading will begin as a trackman; as a recent book says, will want to peasantize himself and fall in love with the soil, machine grease, coal, or cattle. If he is city-bred, he will plunge far into the country; and if a country larrikin, he will go into the city and strive to work to the top. If he is philanthropic, he will go into slum work and its squalor; if he is to teach, he will teach anywhere and anybody; or if he is to be a professor, he will fill half a dozen chairs at once in a monotypic college, because he loves independence and the satisfaction of doing.

How is this attained? In answer, I point to Hampton and some of the half or three-fourths industrial schools for the nation's Indian wards. Nowhere does education work such changes and improvements in so brief a space of time, and it is all because these youths touch life. Here we must find our norm; this is part of the people's college which we must improve on if we can. Personally, I am sometimes proud that I know how to do every kind of old-fashioned farm work; that in my German student days I took lessons so that I can bind, gild, and cover a book; make a shoe and a broom complete, do a little glass-blowing, plumbing, and gold-beating. But my pride is humbled when I see young men who can also make harnesses and saddles; are good blacksmiths; can apply a bandage, and do various kinds of rope-splicing; are amateur wheelwrights, carpenters, and coastguards; can print and do onyx work; understand ice-making, tinning, and electrical machines; are at home in the dairy, poultry yard, and garden; know the rudiments of forestry, bee-keeping, drainage, and photography—this is liberal motor education, and I bow to my masters. They are armed cap-a-pie and come down solidly on all fours, wherever life plants them. This is a part of the liberal education of the future. It gives character and makes men who will make our future social and political institutions in their own image and inspire them with their own soul.

This kind of people's college, with these three elements—English, science, motor training—and others added *ad libitum,* will say to the conservative endowed college of the East which, as is the case with three in New England, still gives no credits whatever in entrance examinations for any degree of proficiency in any of these things save English alone: Here are our graduates; we have done for them the best we could to realize all the possibilities of their golden age. We have given them a taste both of life and of learning; if our graduates can now do better with you than with us, you must take them. We high schools will now organize by ourselves; we know this stage of youth best; we will make our certificate and diploma system the best possible; and if our graduates are articled to you upon our word of honor, that must suffice. We owe you a great debt for training our teachers and for stimulating us in the past. That debt we will now pay, but you must no longer prescribe our work or define our field any more than your own is prescribed. It may be a hard lesson at first, as was yours to us, but it will be no less wholesome; both in numbers and stimulus, your work will improve.

Finally, I am more and more persuaded that in its highest sense teaching ought to be a universal vocation. Guyau says that it should be the only education for women. I would add, and for men as well. Statesmanship, religion, and science all become precious according as they tend to the ever higher development of man. Education involves all other topics, and is that in which the education of all should culminate. The greatest of all reforms are educational reforms, and none others are complete without it. It is the best measure of progress. The philosophy of education is the highest and only philosophy. It is our chief obligation to the future. Its work consists in making an ideal environment for the development of the super-man that is to be; and, while we must train the intellect, the will is far larger and the heart larger yet. Aristotle defined education as teaching men to fear aright; for Jesus it was to teach them to love aright, to fix the affections on the highest and wean them from the lowest. Some have conceived it as teaching men to be angry aright; not to fret at trifles, but to generate torrents of consuming wrath at great abuses; or to pity aright and shape the charity of the heart toward fit objects. In a single word, it is human evolution, and its goal is so to construct experience and knowledge as to advance growth. An age of growth like the present lays upon us new and larger opportunities and duties, and history waits to see if we can develop the wisdom and the vigor which our age demands. It wants not talk, but deeds; not theories, but practical and in some respects radical reconstructions.

IV

Health, Sex, and Morals

"We are soldiers of Christ, strengthening our muscles not against a foreign foe, but against sin within and without us."

10. Christianity and Physical Culture*

Fundamental to Hall's interpretation of natural school-ing was the extraordinary emphasis he placed on healthy bodies and strong, virtuous wills. At a time when a president of the United States, Theodore Roosevelt, was the nation's foremost advocate and practitioner of the "gospel of strenuosity," Hall found an eager response to his pronouncements on the essential link between Christian morals and physical vigor. The following ad-dress on muscular Christianity was delivered in 1901, appropriately, before a meeting of the Young Men's Christian Association.

Health means holiness or wholeness. The words healthy, holy, hale, heal, and whole all come from the same Anglo-Saxon root. Physiological psychology is now re-storing this deep philosophy embedded in the words. In its light let us re-translate some Bible texts—worship the Lord in the beauty of healthfulness; healthfulness be-cometh Thy house O Lord; serve Him in healthfulness; preserve my soul for I am healthful; this is a healthful man of God; the healthful Scriptures, the healthful day, spirit, people, etc. This sums up the new hygiene in the blessed revival of which it is our privilege to live, and which is rescuing mans' body from the still persistent traces of the old ascetic neglect. Ask with reverence, what

* *The Pedagogical Seminary,* IX (September, 1902), 374–378.

shall it profit a man if he gain the whole world of wealth, knowledge and power, and lose his own health; or what shall we give in exchange for health? Without it, the mind tends to grow feeble; the will to be freaky; the heart to lose its courage; virtue to be exotic or a pale cellar plant; and the human brain, the very highest and most complex product of the great biologos in the world, the only mouthpiece of God through which alone he has revealed himself, to become anemic and languid. Jesus is the healer or whole maker, who came to purge the world of sin and disease and give us the soundest hearts and souls in the soundest bodies.

One of the best products of health is abounding joy or euphoria, such as we feel in the rapture of just being alive on a spring morning, when we overflow with the superfluous energy that makes the play spirit in the world purge away the primal curse of work and gives a buoyancy that no pain and affliction can entirely overwhelm. This holy or healthful joy is the end toward which creation strives and is the raw material out of which the special and lower pleasures of sense, of wealth, discovery, gratified ambition and art, are made. Educational and even religious systems are thus measured by the health, wholeness, and holiness they can produce.

Chief among the controllable means to health is wise muscle culture. By weight the adult human body is nearly one-half muscle. The muscles are the only organs of the will and are likely to share its strength or weakness. Muscles have done nearly all man's work in the world. They have tilled the soil, built cities, fought, written all the books, and spoken all the words. Through all the past man has been the striver and toiler. There is a sense in which all good conduct and morality may be defined as right muscle habits. More than this, just in proportion as muscles grow weak and flabby, the chasm between knowing and doing the right, in which so many men are lost, yawns wide and deep; and as they become tense and firm doing becomes—as F. W. Robertson was wont to say it should—the best organ of knowing. Rational muscle culture, therefore, for its moral effects, often for the young the very best possible means of resisting evil and establishing righteousness, is the gospel I preach to-day, a gospel so reinforced by all the new knowledge we are now so rapidly gaining of man's body and his soul, that it is certain to become a dominant note in the pulpit itself, just in proportion as those whose vocation it is to save souls realize that they must study to know what the soul is.

But, alas! how much there is now in modern life that makes for decadence and degeneration of both muscle and health. The city, that great "biological furnace," a new and perhaps chief feature of our day, so contrasted with that of the country where alone man can be fully natural; sedentary life in office and school that favors attitudes of collapses; that reduces the action and even the volume of the lungs and stomach; that is so hard on the heart—itself only a muscle—and the blood vessels, the health of which is so all conditioning; the restriction of the eye, which normally roves freely far and near, to the monotonous zigzag of the printed page, and as the progressive increase of its defects are shown in the saddening statistics; the pallid, muddy or chlorotic complexions, stoop, decaying teeth, premature grayness and baldness; the great increase of nervous disorders; and added to all these, the use of machines which are now suddenly exempting human muscles from the strenuous life which developed them and to which they have been wonted for generations;—this is the situation. But this is not all. We are now coming to know the age of adolescence from the early teens into the early twenties, and we find that one of its chief features, when normal, is muscle growth. It is the age of nature's majority, when the young leave home and begin the great struggle for individual existence. Muscles should now grow both in size and power as never before or after. It is their nascent period of now or never, and should be sacred to their culture for the sake of will and virtue. It is also the age when the strongest of all human passions develops, which exposes it to the greatest of all temptations to sin, and the chief preventative measure to sexual vice is now physical training.

Its neglect is never so dangerous. Careful research shows that the difference in the strength between the weakest and the strongest youth is twice as great in the later teens as in the earlier, and this difference is largely determined by use or disuse. Licentiousness almost immediately reduces strength in a surprising and measurable degree, whereas abundant physical exercise uses the available energy of the body in healthful ways, and reduces temptation in almost inverse ratio. Not only strength, but circulation or irrigation of the tissues with blood is most variable at this age and most dependent upon regimen. Without abundant exercise, the heart which should grow very rapidly in both size and power, remains both small and weak, as does the caliber of the great arteries.

Now physical achievements fire the heart of youth in a way which adults who have not experienced it, find it hard to appreciate. To be "great with hands and feet," an ideal which inspired Pindar who sung the achievements of the Greek athletes, brings just those fervors, calentures and enthusiasms, which are the chief need of youth. Youth must be intense; must tingle and glow; have excitement; stretch lungs, blood vessels, muscles to their greatest capacity by warming up and getting second breath for both mind and body, and this makes for righteousness, because it lessens the power of sin over body and soul.

I have thus stated the need and defined the goal, and now I am called in as an expert, sympathetic but outside enough of the movement to be impartial, to report on the past progress and present state of body training in these Associations. I find that since 1869, when the first gymnasium was opened in New York, over 475 equipped gymnasia, training more than 86,000 young men, have been established in the 610 city or large town associations of the country. Slowly and in the face of much early lack of appreciation and even prejudice and despite many obstacles, the new problems, some of them at first discouraging, have been one after another solved. Physical trainers, at first sometimes chosen from bad surroundings of circus and professionalism, have been trained; well-manned institutions established for this special purpose at Springfield and Chicago; summer sessions, camps and conferences held for further training of leaders; courses of study extended; methods of physical examination steadily improved; experts like Roberts and Gulick, known and honored leaders wherever physical training is studied, and more lately the athletic league of over 100 associations, to still further unify and perfect the work. Among all the marvellous advances of Christianity either within this magnificent organization or without it, in this land and century or any other lands and ages, the future historian of the church of Christ will place this movement of carrying the gospel to the body as one of the most epoch making.

The German Turner system, which sometimes brings 5,000 trained men in the field in this country, exercising in uniform under one command, has been one of the most potent allies of patriotism in the German Fatherland, and for nearly three generations has contributed to improve the bodies and increase the national strength under Jahn's inspiring motto, "only strong muscles can make men great and nations free." For two generations the Swedish system, less national, more specialized, scientific and governmental, has given heart and life to another great racial stock. The English method of play, sports and games expresses the brawn and brain of English life and is both cause and effect of much that is best in our mother country. We seek to combine the spontaneity of the Anglo-Saxon body cult; the science of the Swedish; and the love of country which inspired the Germans, but our loyalty is to a kingdom invisible, not made with hands. The watchword *frisch, frei, froelich, from*[m], shows the dimensions of this all-round movement. We are soldiers of Christ, strengthening our muscles not against a foreign foe, but against sin within and without us. We would bring in a higher kingdom of man, regenerate in body; make it more stalwart, persistent, enduring, taller, with better hearts, stomachs, nerves, and more resistful to man's great enemy—disease.

To one thing I exhort every man and woman who hears my voice. As you, and you, and you, are Christians, live up to the top of your condition; cultivate an appetite for food that is a physical conscience trained to point true to the pole of the needs of the body; train a little every day keeping well within the limits of your vitality and with careful adjustment to your power to recuperate from fatigue; consider your posture, carriage, bearing, and regimen; if you are young learn, if you can and have not, to run a little without initial embarrassment; work or play actively enough every day to draw away the blood from the centers of congestion; study dosage a little or the effects of the same exercises in large and small quantities; if you work with the brain, avoid exercises that involve spurtiness, close attention, or that throw the strain on the nerves. Remember that nowadays at forty, most men are either invalids or philosophers—invalids if they have done their work wrongly or are burned out with vice, individual or hereditary, and philosophers if they have had the rare insight to learn to know themselves so as to keep completely well. It is said of the great thinker, Kant, that he prided himself more upon keeping his frail body alive till eighty, and getting so much work out of it, than upon writing all his volumes. Try these things yourselves faithfully, and you will begin to feel within you this new gospel of the body, the light of which is now being shed abroad in the world as never before.

Men are, happily, just now beginning to learn what a power can be brought to bear against the kingdom of evil in the world by right body keeping; how the body can be built up by patient attention; how we can develop the large fundamental muscles that move the great joints, and as it were lead the energy thus generated down and out to the finer muscles that move the face, vocal organs, fingers, and do the work of skill and precision in the world; how we can give rhythm and cadence to the whole soul life by well adjusted movements, and as it were, like some of the Bible heroes again dance before the Lord in worship; how curative of disease and corrective of deformity well prescribed gymnastics can be; how active muscle habits develop a love of nature and teach sentiment which is sometimes prone to go to waste in gush and vapid enthusiasms, to harness itself to do the work of the world; and what a sin and shame it is when our temples of the Holy Ghost are neglected and lapse to premature decay.

Finally, this is a world and age of achievement. Men are coming to be measured more and more not by what they know or even what they feel, important as that is, but by what they can do and actively accomplish in the world. Knowledge can never save individuals or nations. Subjective emotions are not enough. But there is one language and one only of complete manhood, and that is willed action, and it is to make our lives speak in this language and thus to make them historic that we train, what psychology now sees to be the chief power in man, the will, the only organs of which are muscles.

11. Sex Education*

Hall broached the relations between sex and psychology at a time when Victorian strictures on the subject had not yet given way to the relative freedom of discussion that marked the 1920's. Fully recognizing the dangers of misunderstanding on this delicate issue, Hall nevertheless insisted on dealing with it. In the first place, he thought sex, like all other aspects of man's physical nature, more divine than degrading. Moreover, he was persuaded that better understanding of the sexual function was essential to the biological evolution of the race, as his allusions to the eugenics movement suggest. No more than Sigmund Freud, however, was Hall an advocate of sexual license. This selection indicates that he was searching for ways in which the school might delay sexual development and channel sexual drives into socially acceptable behavior.

The 1,500,000,000 people, more or less, alive on the earth to-day are but a mere handful compared with the countless generations who are to proceed from their loins in the future. All posterity slumbers now in our bodies, as we did in our ancestors. They demand of us the supreme right and blessing of being well born, and they will have

* "The Needs and Methods of Educating Young People in the Hygiene of Sex," *The Pedagogical Seminary,* XV (March, 1908), 82–91. This paper was originally read before the American Society of Sanitary and Moral Prophylaxis.

only curses for us if they awaken into life handicapped by our errors. Their interests should dominate all our lives, for that is living for the children, for our duty of all duties is to transmit the sacred torch of life undimmed, and if possible a little brightened, to our children's children in *saecula saeculorum*. This is the chief end of man and of woman. The welfare of all this cloud of witnesses is committed to our honor and virtue. The basis of the new biological ethics of to-day and of the future is that everything is right that makes for the welfare of the yet unborn and all is wrong that injures them, and to do so is the unpardonable sin—the only one nature knows. Just as the soma and all the mortal cells and organs of the body and all their activities throughout our individual lives are only to serve the deathless germ plasm, so every human institution, home, school, state, church and all the rest exist primarily in order to bring children and youth on and up to their highest possible maturity of body and soul and the value not only of all institutions, but of art, science, literature, culture and civilization itself are ultimately measured and graded by how much they contribute to this supreme end. Our religion began in the promise to and covenant with Abraham that if he lived aright his seed should be as the stars of heaven for multitude, and the essence of Christianity was the effort to fix the highest of all human sentiments upon the loftiest of all objects and thus to bring salvation by ennobling love. Hence, both Testaments are in a sense a continued love story, the romance of humanity with God. On this view, if we say that God himself when biologically interpreted is simply posterity personified, he would again be worthy of the supreme reverence, devotion and service of those who are now prone to neglect and forget him.

Now the aberrant fallen aspect of man, wherein he differs from all animals, is rooted in the excessive development of the sex functions which is no longer limited to breeding seasons nor to the desire of the female, nor exercised for procreation only, but has become an end in itself. Man is prone to mortgage posterity by consuming in his own self-gratification energies that belong to the future, or in Herbert Spencer's phrase, to over-magnify individuation at the cost of genetic powers, for there is in all a critical point beyond which development of the ego robs the future. Our life is like a richly laden ship of which we are simply the steersmen with the sole duty of navigating our bark from the last safely on to the next generation, but over-self-indulgence is breaking into the hold and looting the cargo to the loss of the consignees, our children. Like fire, sex is a good servant but a tyrannous master, and how few are they to-day entirely unscathed either by its conflagrations or its smoldering inner calentures. Prostitution, abortion, preventives, precocity, sex diseases, divorces, defective parenthood, race suicide, inability to nurse, declining birthrate in every country in Western and Central Europe and still more so in this country for native born population—all these are only a few of the more salient outcrops of the one great fact of growing abnormality of the sex function which some anthropologists now think marks the same stage of race senescence as began the decline and fall of the great nations of old.

However this may be, men have learned very much about sex within the last two decades, so that we can now begin at least to take a broad comparative view of it from its origin up to the highest animals, including man. The studies of all its grossest perversities, repulsive as they are, have shed very precious light, while just now such studies as those of Freud, Jung, Bleuler, Riklin and others in Germany, and Janet and his group in France, have shown its profound and often all-conditioning psychic ramifications and immensely broadened the field of hysteria, essentially rejustifying its etymology, though finding its symptoms often well developed in men. We have learned, too, how sex has permeated all religions, the chief problem of which some are now boldly saying always has been and must be to regulate and explain sex in its wider relationships, and thus including not merely phallic types of worship which once covered the world, but even the religion of totemic clans by their rules of exogamy. From all these sources new data are rather suddenly at hand for a far deeper and broader knowledge of sex than ever before, and this seems now certain to rescue the subject from the sex intoxicated mystics and from the tendency of even sane men to become dogmatic, extravagant, if not absurd upon this subject as upon no other.

The old prudery and false reticence, too, are giving way all along the line. Not only are novels, drama and often works of art entering this field more freely, whether for good or ill, but staid professors like Ehrenfels of Prague, are developing a radically new sex ethics, while Galton's eugenic schemes involve the endowment of wedlock for the fit if found to be so when examined by a medical commission. The vigorous group of young professors who support the German archive for racial and social biology are urging legislation to unsex or otherwise eliminate reproduction by the unfit but extremely fecund Jukes, Sebalds, Buddenbrucks [Buddenbrooks] and other degenerate families, to compel marriage of all fit by progressive fines designed to make the way of the capable bachelors hard and their selfishness opprobrious.

Somer and half a dozen others backed by a society are working out tirelessly very elaborate pedigrees of royal and other families to draw therefrom lessons for practical human stirpiculture. European countries, conscious of their dwindling birthrate and the increasing rate of infant mortality during the first year, as well as of the tide of emigration to both Americas, are now intensely alive to the necessity of having more men for their armies, their industries and their colonies, and that in the competition between different countries natural supremacy will ultimately go to that country that is most fecund— hence they are farther on than we in the study of these larger problems of sex, and many startling schemes designed to produce more and better men and women are already being discussed.

In the Mannheim Conference on sex pedagogy in 1905, the proceedings of which have only just appeared in a stately volume, not one voice dissented from the proposition that sex should be taught in the later years of secondary boys' schools, and the only grave differences of opinion were as to what should be taught, how and by whom, and whether certain instruction should not begin some years earlier and as to whether and how girls should be taught. In Finland, Switzerland and Hungary such instruction has been for some years authorized by law and it has also been given in a dozen or more of the largest German cities and with best results, although the Prussian cultus minister [minister of culture] has not formally sanctioned it. Of course parents should do it, but very few will and can, although many courses in Germany are now offered to educate them in that duty. To believe or to urge, as is often done, that children now and here come up to the age of twelve or even ten to-day innocent of all sex knowledge is simply ignorance. City life itself makes knowledge more precocious and school associations suddenly increase it so that our censuses indicate that the vast majority of children of eight or ten already have quite a body of misinformation that is most eagerly sought, that is gross in form and deplorably misleading in content. Wherever special studies have been made they indicate, too, that nearly every boy before the end of the teens has at least experimented with himself, knows a good stock of indecent words and stories and a large percentage of them, despite the noble work of the purity agencies, have soiled their minds with literature that it is a crime to print or circulate, have dangerously false views about the dangers and gravity of disease, the need of indulgence, while many are more or less panicky about their spontaneous nocturnal experiences and a percentage variously estimated from three to twelve have written to quacks whose flaunting scare advertisements many newspapers still print; and all this while mothers and lady teachers are living on complacently in their fools' paradise confident that all is well with their callow adolescent darlings, so secret, subterranean and spun-over with the web of lies and deceits is sexual life.

Our life fortunately begins with a sexually neuter period during which no sex consciousness exists, a stage typically illustrated by the four-year-old boy's question how could one tell when children were in bathing with their clothes off which were boys and which were girls? Of course the age of primeval innocence should be prolonged by every possible means, and the only sex hygiene is cleanliness to avoid irritation, loose and not too warm clothing, wholesome food, open bowels, regularity, cool bedding, active life, and objective interests. Knowledge on this subject should be given only as interest arises, and to force it prematurely at this or any other stage is a kind of psychic rape, and makes directly for precocity, so that eager curiosity should always be assured before information is given. Self handling at this age is exceptional and needs medical care.

The second specific interest which seems usually to nearly coincide with school age, is where babies come from, when the myth of the stork, doctor, or the milkman is outgrown. This is the stage Helen Keller was in when her teacher exclaimed that she was tired of hearing of new little cows, cats, dogs, babies, and when she asked the meaning of the word born, and also a group of school girls of eight to eleven who wrote and signed a round robin request to the teacher to tell them where men and women come from. In most cases it is enough at first to explain that the young grow in the mother's body and in due time are brought forth, and that this is true of animals as well as men.

Of course the mother should give this information simply, briefly, and as something rather mysterious and sacred, though but few mothers do so, so that the teacher must qualify for this task. All that is necessary can be told briefly, and it ought to be personal. Of course, pedagogically, it should come incidentally in the nature study course, but so important is it that of itself it is a sufficient motive to introduce the subject of rudimentary zoölogy in the middle grammar grades. The needs of the sexes, of course, differ here, and it would be advantageous to segregate them for this instruction. The ideal is a woman teacher for girls and a man for boys. This would appeal far more to girls than to boys before puberty. I cannot yet find any course or text which seems to me quite ideal, although I have collected many, and Germany has at least one, and perhaps three, that are in many respects admirable.

The paternal function excites interest much later, and how to teach it many think a pedagogic crux. If the child really did repeat the history of the race this would come far later, but with our precocious sexual éclaircissement which presents this in the very worst light and long before its time, something has to be done on the back fire or immunization principle. The fertilization of plants and flowers by insects and the wind is a familiar prelude, and this knowledge when sex begins to bourgeon in the soul will blossom out with new significance. So fertilization of lower animals, of those that lay eggs, of the relations between sperm cell and ova on up the scale can be brought in an enlightening way without too objective diagrams of human organs or processes as some advocate, for the child's mind is very alert to see and apply all needed lessons from lower forms, so close are its relations to, and sympathies with, animal life. The normal should, of course, always precede the abnormal, and animal courtship, brooding, etc., are normal. This instruction need not be prolonged or much methodized and if rightly taught does not need to be examined on. Here too much illustration, amplification and detail hinders understanding, while sex segregation is still more desirable, though where it is not practical this should not prevent teaching the subject, even to mixed classes just before puberty.

With the dawn of adolescence, when the sexes naturally draw more or less apart in the home, games, and socially, and when in nearly all savage races boys and girls are given instruction apart, often lasting for weeks, and with very impressive ceremonial initiation into manhood (for instruction in sex and its irradiation constitutes most of the material of savage education) the chief need of girls is for hygienic instruction concerning their monthly regimen at an age when folly and ignorance are most dangerous. The needs of boys are now several; first, to know the harmfulness of self-abuse, which is very grave, although it has been the fashion to exaggerate it. They must also be disabused of their morbid fears of being lost because of the spontaneous nocturnal experiences which quacks know so well how to prey upon. Third, they need some plain talk about the dangers of infection, both by black plague and by gonorrhea and the enormous evils of the latter, which are only lately adequately understood. All this instruction should, to be authoritative, be given by a physician. Boys are not much impressed by goody talks about purity such as clergymen, teachers or principals, and the worst of all, ladies are likely to give, and such as are now quite the fashion in the great English schools Eaton [Eton], Harrow, Rugby, etc., where such preachments are known in school slang as "smut jaws." I believe boys of fourteen need to be told, too, of the marvellous nature of the germ plasm, the most complex and highest product of the great biologos or spirit of life, and how the sexual glands in man best take care of their own functions and are no more prone to atrophy from disuse than are the lacrimal glands. They should be informed rather fully of the dangers and also the results of infection. After every general talk there should be a very carefully devised opportunity and encouragement for personal conferences that the sexual fears, that often become perfect obsessions, be removed, that more instruction be given to individuals who need it, etc. The physical trainer should weigh, measure and test heart, lungs, muscles, always incidentally observing sex, and co-operate according to need with the medical instructor, unless he can give such instruction himself. Stripping periodically before an expert is as salutary today as it was in ancient Sparta, and from it many most wholesome influences can be evolved. So much I think the State now owes to every fourteen-year-old boy, and if we begin with those of eighteen, as we should do without delay, such instruction would be sure to gravitate downward to the very beginning of puberty, when its benefits were seen. In Germany, a few have advocated teaching sex perversions, even Sadism, Masochism, fetichism, pediastry, and even some pornologic details, and one text including these things has been prepared there. Curiously, in Germany, it is women teachers who advocate most unreserved teaching, but I believe all this is entirely wrong, unless, of course, individually where perverse tendencies are already indicated.

For the high school Cohen and Rohleder in Germany and various investigators in England and France think self-abuse among boys the rule and perfect chastity the rare exception, while Blaschko's careful statistics of German university students convince him that they show "a greater proportion of sex infection than any other class in the community." In this country reliable and comprehensive statistics are wanting. Certain it is that sedentary student life with its too common exemption from hard work, mental or physical, more is the pity, sheltered as it is from the struggle for existence, predisposes to temptation. The very causes that make boys leave high school and that fill college with those who do not expect to make their living by what they learn there —football, athleticism, liberty—young barbarians at play have influence here. Collegiate instruction in this subject is surely imperative, and in this great stress should be laid upon the sense of honor, chivalry and respect to women; on the gross egotism and dishonor of seduction in ways so almost ideally set forth by the lectures to students of Professor Ziegler of Strassburg and in France by Wagner. Students before college need to be told of the wide range and variation of organs, both in form, size and functional activity within the limits of normality, for physical examiners agree in reporting that many, if not most, young men pass through a stage of anxiety and sometimes of morbid fears lest they are hopelessly abnormal.

All girls before leaving the secondary schools should be told of the commonest wiles and arguments used for their betrayal and some think as to risks, dangers and degrees of permissible liberty. Girls' intuitions, however, are wiser and more reliable and they need less instruction upon most of these topics, save the last, than boys. The preponderance of opinion seems to be against either instructing girls in advance what to do if unfortunate, etc., or boys concerning the proper course if they become infected and is unanimous against information concerning precautions against either of these calamities.

To me it seems clear that all children should have some instruction in this subject suitable to their age before they satisfy the requirements of school attendance and that this should be given by qualified instructors of the same sex. Hence every normal school should train teachers in this field. The church, too, has a duty in this respect which it is happily just beginning to realize in a few places. Extension schoolhouse lectures should be offered to mothers and also to fathers, as they should in most young people's clubs and societies, Christian Endeavorers, Epworth Leagues, Young Men's Christian Association and the now very many other associations for the young, of whatever faith. Such instruction should not be prolonged or over-systematic, for the pedagogic method here needed is entirely unique. Every child ought to be in frank and confidential relation with some wise, older mentor, the parent of course preferred, to whom it can and will freely turn during all the ten or more years before maturity. Of the two or three score books designed for the young on these topics in my collection every one seems to me too large and diffuse and holds the mind too long upon the subject, while most were written by people with more zeal than knowledge and often with more knowledge than discretion.

But finally, medical knowledge, indispensable as it is, is not enough, but the prophylactic needed is vastly larger. Nature's method is to long-circuit and evolve ever more widely irradiating secondary sex qualities, plumes, wattles, antlers, organs of offense and defense, balzing and tumbling and all the varieties of love antics and the showing-off instinct that are involved in the function of sexual selection. So many, if not most, of the best qualities of the human body and mind are built upon the basis of sex, and from which evolve deportment, manners, dress, ornament, the spirit of personal loyalty and devotion, the antique idea of friendship, the sentiment of honor, and above all, the nobler and purer expressions of love, and even religion itself, so that it is plain that whatever strengthens these tends to sublimate, spiritualize and normalize sex. The ideals of body keeping, physical perfection and strength, agility, skill, beauty, the full development of shoulders, chest, arms, loins, legs, a ruddy cheek, clear eye, love of exercise, of cold water and cleanliness, of nature afield, of contest and competition involving victory and defeat, the legitimate ambition of being a splendid animal with a strong and flexible voice, defiance of wind and weather, a normal appetite and sane regular sleeping habits, hearty, free, open manners, a love of the Turner's ideal—"frisch, frei, fröhlich, fromm"—a laudable passion to excel, a love of rhythmical movements as exemplified in periods of history when dancing was most varied and vigorous and did most to cadence the soul to virtue and preform it for religion; those who know, feel, do these things are developing probably the most effective of all checks and come thus against every kind of sexual aberration. It is incalculably harder to develop these results than it is to give a few lectures on sex dangers, but it is as much more effective as it is harder. It is these things in which the sexually corrupt are crippled and here those who know too much of Venusberg cannot enter. If this is so, then every introduction of a motor element in place of the old sedentary modes of training makes for chastity.

So the intelligence of youth is normally keen, alert, curious, sprouting all over with eager spontaneous interests, grasping out for new facts, fond of trying its new found powers of reason by argumentation and dispute, ambitious for the summit like the hero of Longfellow's Excelsior, showing now amazing spells of concentration, perseverance, though perhaps alternating with periods of distraction and unrest. So every intellectual interest is a sedative, or perhaps better, an alternative of the sensuous side of sex, while merely formal school topics, dull teaching, listless routine, zestless attention are almost of themselves temptations to passion which always presses for entrance into unoccupied minds and moments and wherever there are unused functions tends to sap them. The deeds and words of great men are never so inspiring, and teachers and courses that fail of this are co-respondents with the lusty blood of youth in the indictment of sexual errors now brought against students. Among the many reasons for the more practical and even occupational training of boys I count this moral one as one of the chief because the contact with life it brings rouses a sense of responsibility to both self and the community and makes the call of the future louder and all this has a sex value perhaps primary and at least secondary.

Again, puberty is the birthday of the feelings and emotions, and these are the older and most dominant parts of the soul that really rule all our lives and have very much to do in determining sanity and insanity. Young people need to glow, tingle and crepitate with sentiments, and the appetite for excitement and sensation is at its height in the teens and here is where the principle of vicariousness of Aristotelian catharsis comes in and gives the teacher of higher sexology his chief opportunity and resource. Excitement, the young must and will have, for the feelings are now in their very life. If they cannot find it in the worthy, they are strongly predisposed to seek it in the grosser forms of pleasure. Hence, every glow of aesthetic appreciation for a great work of art, every thrill aroused by an act of sublime heroism, every pulse of religious aspiration weakens by just so much the potential energy of passion because it has found its kinetic equivalent in a higher form of expression. It is for this reason that some of our German co-laborers on this theme have advocated a carefully selected course of love stories chosen so as to bring out the highest, most chivalric side of the tender passion at the age when it is most capable of idealization, and still more in that country and now lately here have seen the necessity of encouraging theatre going to plays palpitating with life, action and adventure that emotional tension may be discharged not merely harmlessly but in a way elevating in the middle teens. Even melodrama, gushy and tawdry though it may seem to adults, has been sometimes authorized. The statistical studies lately made of children's attendance upon and love of the theatre as well as of their passion for assuming rôles of many kinds in ever so fragmentary a way have come to us pedagogues of late almost as the revelation of a new power in human nature, the educational utilization of which when we learn how to do the most and best with it, will be comparable to the harnessing of a new power of nature into the service of man.

To conclude, I am convinced that if religion were known to be only a myth and a superstition by cultured adults, it would have to be kept and its function modified for the young because of its prophylactic value for this function, even if it had no other. Its great themes are life, death, virtue, sin, duty and responsibility, love and service of God and man. These awaken old phylogenetic echoes in the youthful soul which bring it into salutary rapport with the past of the race in which, if evolution is true, the best has survived and the worst perished. Those who have been most truly religious have most sought purity and alliance with the power that works righteousness. The chief sin of the world is in the sphere of sex, and the youthful struggle with temptation here is the only field where the hackneyed expressions of being corrupt, polluted, lost, and then rejuvenated, of being in the hands of a power stronger than human will become literally true. Especially if the theme of the religion of the future be the relation of the individual to the race and to posterity, and if the world to-day is increasingly in need of a new dispensation of sexual theory and practice, we shall have to have a national, industrial, social, political as well as religious revival, such as the world has seen but once or possibly twice since the Renaissance. If this ever comes, it can only spring from a sense of demerit intensified almost to the point of moral despair and this, folk psychology shows us, can only arise from a conviction of impending racial decadence and sterility. This, I believe, we cannot expect because we have already begun to glimpse the magnitude and importance of this subject from so many sides and to work against downward tendencies so that what we must look forward to is a reform and progress that will come by methods of evolution and not those of revolution.

12. Coeducation in the High School*

Concern over early sexual development led Hall to undertake a vigorous though largely futile campaign against coeducation in the high school. Because nature brings about the marked differentiation of the sexes at puberty, Hall argued, an education according to nature should preserve and heighten the differences by separating adolescent boys and girls. In the article reprinted here, he characteristically interprets female emancipation as freedom from masculine ideals rather than freedom to share them.

Men and women differ in their dimension, sense, tissue, organ, in their abilities, in crime, disease; and these differences, which science is now multiplying and emphasizing, increase with advancing civilization. In savagery women and men are more alike in their physical structure and in their occupations, but with real progress the sexes diverge and draw apart, and the diversities always present are multiplied and accentuated. Intersexual differences culminate during the sexual period. Little boys and girls play together, do the same things, in many respects have the same tastes, are unconscious of sex, as too in senescence there is reapproximation. Old men and women become more like each other and are again in a sense sexless.

* National Educational Association, *Addresses and Proceedings,* *1903,* pp. 446–451.

Divergence is most marked and sudden in the pubescent period—in the early teens. At this time, by almost world-wide consent, boys and girls separate, and lead their lives during this most critical period of inception more or less apart, at least for a few years, until the ferment of mind and body which results in maturity of functions then born and culminating in nubility has done its work. The family and the home abundantly recognize this tendency. At twelve or fourteen brothers and sisters develop a life more independent of each other than before. Their home occupations differ, as do their plays, games, tastes. This is normal and biological. What our school and other institutions should do is to push distinctions to their uttermost, to make boys more manly and girls more womanly. We should respect the law of sexual differences, and not forget that motherhood is a very different thing from fatherhood. Neither sex should copy or set patterns to the other, but all parts should be played harmoniously and clearly in the great sex symphony.

I have here nothing to say against coeducation in college, still less in university grades after the maturity which comes at eighteen or twenty has been achieved; but it is high time to ask ourselves whether the theory and practice of identical coeducation, which has lately been carried to a greater extreme in this country than the rest of the world recognizes, has not brought certain grave dangers; whether it does not interfere with the natural differentiations everywhere seen in home and society. I recognize, of course, the great argument of economy. We should save money and effort, could we unite churches of not too diverse creeds; could give better preaching, music, improve the edifice, etc. I am by no means ready to advocate the abolition of coeducation, but my purpose today is to sum up in a rough, brief way our account of profit and loss with it.

On the one hand, I believe that each sex best develops some of its own best qualities in the presence of the other; but the question still remains: How much? when? and in what way? Association secures this end. I think that girls and boys are often interested in different aspects of the same topic, and this may have a tendency to broaden the view-point of each and bring it into sympathy with that of the other; but the question still remains whether one be not too much attracted to the sphere of the other. No doubt some girls become a little less gushy and sentimental, their conduct more thoughtful; their sense of responsibility for one of woman's great functions, which is bestowing praise, is increased. There is much evidence that certain boys' vices are mitigated; they are made more urbane; thoughts of sex are made more healthful. In some respects boys are stimulated to good scholarship by girls, who in many schools and topics excel them. We should ask, however, what nature's way is at this stage of life; whether boys, in order to be well verified later, ought to be so boisterous and even rough as to be at times unfit companions for girls; or whether, on the other hand, girls, to be best matured, ought not to have their sentimental periods of instability, especially when we venture to raise the question, whether for a girl in the early teens, when her health for her whole life depends upon normalizing the lunar month, there is not something unhygienic, un-natural, not to say a little monstrous, in school associations with boys when she must suppress and conceal her instincts, feelings, and instinctive promptings, and these times which suggest withdrawing, stepping aside to let Lord Nature do its beautiful, magnificent work of efflorescence. It is a sacred time of reverent exemption from the hard struggle of existence in the world, mental effort in the school. Medical specialists, many of the best of whom now insist that she thru this should be, as it were, "turned out to grass," or should lie fallow so far as intellectual efforts go, one-fourth the time no doubt, often go too far; but their unanimous voice should not entirely be disregarded.

It is not of this, however, that I would speak, but of the effects of too familiar relations, and especially of the identical work, treatment, and environment of the modern school.

We have now at least eight good and independent statistical studies which show that the ideals of boys from ten years on are almost always those of their own sex, while girls' ideals are increasingly of the opposite sex, or also of men. That the ideals of pubescent girls are not found in great and noble women of the world, or in their literature, but more and more in men, suggests a diversity "between the ideals adopted and the line of life best suited to the interests of the race," and also that we are not furnished in our public schools with adequate womanly ideals in history or literature. The new love of freedom and fame which women have lately felt has produced a reaction toward the other extreme, which inclines girls to abandon the home for the office. "It surely can hardly be called an ideal education for women that permits eighteen out of one hundred college girls to state boldly that they would rather be men than women." More than one-half of the schoolgirls in these censuses choose male ideals, as if those of femininity are disintegrating. A recent writer, in view of this fact, states that "unless there is a change of trend we shall soon have a female sex without a female character." In the progressive feminization of our schools most teachers, perhaps naturally and necessarily, have more or less masculine ideals, and this does not encourage the development of those that constitute the glory of womanhood. "At every age from eight to sixteen girls named from three to twenty more ideals than boys." All these facts indicate a condition of diffused interests and lack of clear-cut purposes, and a need of integration.

When we turn to boys, the case is different. In most public high schools girls preponderate, especially in the upper classes; and in many of them the boys that remain are practically in a girls' school, sometimes taught chiefly, if not solely, by women teachers, at an age when strong men should be in control more than at any other period of life. Boys need a different discipline and moral regimen and atmosphere. They also need a different method of work. Girls excel them in learning, memorization, excepting studies upon suggestion or authority, but are often quite at sea when set to make tests and experiments that give individuality, which is one of the best things in boyhood, a chance to express itself. Girls preponderate in high-school Latin and algebra, because custom and tradition, and perhaps advice, incline them to it. They preponderate in English and history classes more often, let us say, from inner inclination. The boy sooner grows restless in a curriculum where form takes precedence over content. He revolts at much method with meager matter. He craves utility; and when all these instincts are denied, without knowing what is the matter, he drops out of school; when if a robust tone and a true boy life prevailed, such as is found at Harrow, Eton, and Rugby, he would have fought it thru and done well. This feminization of the school spirit, discipline, and personnel is bad for boys. Of course, on the whole perhaps they are made more gentlemanly, at ease, their manners improved; and all this to a woman teacher seems excellent; but something is the matter with the boy in the early teens who can be truly called "a perfect gentleman." That should come later, when the brute and animal element have had opportunity to work themselves off in a healthful normal way. They still have football to themselves, and are the majority perhaps in chemistry, and sometimes in physics; but there is danger of a settled eviration.

The segregation which even our schools are now attempting is always in some degree necessary for full and complete development. Just as the boys' language is apt to creep in and to roughen that of the girls, so girls' interests, ways, standards, and tastes, which are crude at this age, often attract boys out of their orbit. While some differences are emphasized by contact, others are compromised. Boys tend to grow content with mechanical memorata work, and, excelling on the lines of girls' qualities, fail to develop those of their own. There is a little charm and bloom rubbed off the ideal of girlhood by close contact, and boyhood seems less ideal to the girls at close range. In place of the mystic attraction of the other sex that has inspired so much that is best in the world, familiar comradery brings a little disenchantment. The impulse to be at one's best in the presence of the other sex grows lax, and each comes to feel itself seen thru, so that there is less motive to indulge in the ideal conduct which such contact inspires, because the call for it is incessant.

This disillusioning weakens the motivation to marriage, sometimes on both sides. When girls grow careless in their dress and too negligent of their manners—the best school of morals—and when boys lose all restraint which the presence of girls usually enforces, there is a subtle deterioration. Thus I believe, altho of course it is impossible to prove, that this is one of the factors of a decreasing percentage of marriage among educated young men and women.

At eighteen or twenty the girl normally reaches this maturity, when her ideas of life are amazingly keen and true; when, if her body is developed, she can endure a great deal; when she is nearest, perhaps, the ideal of feminine beauty and perfection. We have lately in this country and Europe had a dozen books, of a more or less naïve or else confessional character, written by girls of this age, showing the first glorious inflorescence of womanly genius and power. In our environment, however, there is little danger that, this age once well past, there will slowly arise a slight sense of aimlessness or lassitude, unrest, uneasiness, as if one were almost unconsciously feeling along the wall for a door to which the key was not at hand. Thus some lose their bloom and, yielding to the great danger of young womanhood, slowly lapse to an anxious state of expectancy, or they desire something not within reach; and so the diathesis of anxiety slowly supervenes. The best thing about college life for girls is, perhaps, that it postpones this incipient disappointment; but it is a little pathetic to read, as I have lately done, the class letters of hundreds of girl graduates, out of college one, two, or three years, turning a little to art, music, travel, teaching, charity work, or trying to find something to which they can devote themselves—some cause, movement, occupation, where their glorious capacity for altruism and self-sacrifice can find a field. The tension is almost imperceptible, perhaps quite unconscious. It is everywhere overborne by a keen interest in

life, by a desire to know the world at first hand, while sus-
ceptibilities are at their height. The apple of intelligence
has been plucked at perhaps a little too great a cost of
health. The purely mental has not been quite suffi-
ciently kept back. They wish to know a good deal
more of the world and to perfect their own personalities, and they would not marry, altho every cell
of their bodies and every unconscious impulse point to
just that end. Soon—it may be in five or ten years or
more—the complexion of ill-health is seen in these
notes; or else life has been adjusted to independence
and self-support.

But I must be brief. What should be done? We can,
at least, enlarge the elective system and wait for
spontaneous interest and needs to declare themselves
even yet more fully; but we must not forget that this has
its limits. Already we have the complaint that where one
sex preponderates in a subject it tends to be avoided by
the other. Again, we can multiply high schools for girls,
and study and utilize their conclusions and experiences
to fit them to their nature and needs, as boys' schools
have been adjusted to theirs. Already we have suggestions of a girls' botany, biology, and chemistry,
emphasizing different methods and topics from those
that prevail today. Again, we can investigate the
suggestion of two kinds of schools for girls: one for those
who wish to follow the principle of training for a
support, leaving motherhood, if it comes, to take care
of itself; and the other, for those who would be trained
first for motherhood and home life, which come to the
vast majority of women, developing a curriculum on this
basis, which is as different from the agenic and agamic
principle as one sex is from the other. At all events, we
must utterly eradicate the now prevalent idea of

intersexual competition. There is no war of sex against sex, and by imagining one, woman has brought great hardship upon us.

Lastly, we must pass beyond the purely personal type of discussion of this topic to which men, and especially women, are too prone. If statistics show that the majority of college women do not marry, and that those who do marry have few children, it is irrelevant to detail the case of Mrs. A. who bore twelve children, reared them all to maturity, and died herself at the age of eighty-six. If anthropology shows that in general women less often specialize, and, where they do so, later by several years than men, it is not necessary to point to the brilliant women who have shown precocious signs of genius and have had great careers. If in every race, and by the concurrent testimony of biology and medicine, women need periods of rest, it is no refutation to sight [*sic*] the women who declare that they have never known pain, ill-health, or remission of a strenuous life at these times.

In fine, my conviction is that woman needs the best. She has won, by almost universal consent, the battle of equal opportunities and privileges. The world and posterity now wait with growing concern to see whether she will be able to face the next and far higher problem of selecting from all the fields now open which interest decrees to be her own, or be content with a second best, with man-made methods, and, lapsing to a cheap idolatry of intellect, forget that she better than man represents the feeling instincts which are higher, deeper, and broader than mere mental culture; that she is a generic being, nearer to the race; that every individual of her sex is a better representative of it; and that the real solution of her problem is in the future.

CHARLES E. STRICKLAND, Assistant Professor of History and Teacher Education at Emory University, was born in Amarillo, Texas, in 1930. He received his B.S. from Southwest Missouri State College and his M.S. and Ph.D. from the University of Wisconsin, where he taught the history of education before joining the faculty of Emory.

CHARLES BURGESS, Assistant Professor of History of Education at the University of Washington, was born in Portland, Oregon, in 1932. He received his B.A. from the University of Oregon and his M.S. and Ph.D. from the University of Wisconsin. Professor Burgess is the author of *Nettie Fowler McCormick: Profile of an American Philanthropist* (1962).